Lifelines

This book is dedicated to all those Christians
I have met, wherever I have travelled, who
want their faith to make a difference.

LIFELINES
SEIZING THE OPPORTUNITY
TO SHARE YOUR FAITH

Mike Hill

The Bible Reading Fellowship
OPENING THE BIBLE

Text copyright © Michael A. Hill 1997

The author asserts the moral right to be
identified as the author of this work.

Published by
The Bible Reading Fellowship
Peter's Way, Sandy Lane West
Oxford OX4 5HG
ISBN 0 7459 2528 6
Albatross Books Pty Ltd
PO Box 320, Sutherland
NSW 2232, Australia
ISBN 0 7324 1560 8

First edition 1997
10 9 8 7 6 5 4 3 2 1 0

Acknowledgments
Unless otherwise stated, scripture quotations are
taken from the New Revised Standard Version of
the Bible copyright © 1989 by the Division of
Christian Education of the National Council of
the Churches of Christ in the USA.

Scripture marked (NIV) is taken from the Holy
Bible, New International Version, copyright ©
1973, 1978, 1984 by International Bible Society.
Used by permission.

A catalogue record for this book is
available from the British Library

Printed and bound in Great Britain
by Cox and Wyman Limited, Reading

CONTENTS

FOREWORD

Slowly but surely the Church is getting the message: evangelism is not an isolated activity but part of a three-fold cord with spirituality and apologetics. One of the strengths of Mike Hill's latest book is that it assumes this throughout. Mike is no mere theorist. He is also a practitioner. In *Lifelines* he offers us a useful tool which roots us in scripture, prods us to pray and encourages us to take action. Many objections to belief in God and Christian faith are honestly faced. Real problems are tackled with frankness and honesty.

This book is born of much experience, both in 'secular work' and Church ministry; first as a parish priest and latterly as an archdeacon. Its accessible style reflects the author himself who is a man of sensitive directness and practical spirituality. It has been my privilege to work with Mike as a friend and colleague over the last few years. From that partnership I have learned much about Christian discipleship. Those who face up to the hard-hitting challenges of this book will find that faith sharing becomes more exciting and that this in turn leads to a deeper love for the Lord who truly is our Lifeline.

Colin Bennetts
Bishop of Buckingham
Co-Chairman of the Archbishops' Springboard Initiative

ACKNOWLEDGMENTS

The task of writing a book is not something I find easy. I have repeatedly thought that this will be the very last time I embark on such an endeavour. It is appropriate, therefore, that I offer my heartfelt thanks to those whose support, encouragement and infinite patience have helped me to achieve the goal of writing this book.

I feel a debt of gratitude to those people who have encouraged me to keep going on days when I have felt like giving up. Some of them are my friends, others are people I hardly know who have felt that the purpose of the book was something worth persevering with. Some of them have had the dubious pleasure of hearing me preach on some of these themes, and have encouraged me to put them down on paper. On reflection, I think I might never have completed the task without their, often inadvertent, encouragement.

There are those whose individual contributions to the task are worthy of specific mention. The Bible Reading Fellowship have been gracious enough to invest in the concept. In particular, one of their commissioning editors, Sue Doggett, should be thanked, not only for her constructive and creative interventions, but especially for her patience!

Claire Rose, with whom I worked for a number of years, has given me exceptional support in getting this book together. Not only has she deciphered my scripts and typed them, but she has exercised her skills in transforming the writings of a speaker into the writings of a writer. In that sense the book is a team effort.

Finally, I am aware that it is not easy to share a home with someone who, on top of all the other things he has to do, is constantly trying to find extra time in order to write. I would therefore like to thank my wife, Anthea, and my five children, Naomi, Charis, Nicholas, Alexa and Lella, who have patiently put up with me and enabled me to write this book.

Michael A. Hill
October 1996

INTRODUCTION

'You are the salt of the earth.'

Matthew 5:13

Robert Warren in his mid-term report on the Decade of Evangelism makes a point that I suspect many of us are aware of. Writing under the heading 'the unfinished agenda', he states the following: '... whilst getting evangelism onto the agenda of the Church, the Decade has not yet got the good news onto the lips of church members in any great measure. That must be a priority for the second half of the Decade.'[1]

I believe that deep down many Christians would love to play a part in helping others to find a faith in Christ. The problem appears to be that many of us don't know how to go about the task. In our offices, schools, hospitals and homes we allow opportunities to pass by rather than take on a conversation that might leave us wanting. The net result is that our impact upon the world is negligible.

The apostle Peter encouraged the recipients of his Epistle to give the reason 'for the hope that is in you'.[2] I realize that this verse is frequently quoted at today's Church and my primary purpose in doing so is to demonstrate that Peter's wisdom is both timely for us *and* strategically sound. It is now widely accepted that when most people are asked how they became Christians they indicate a high degree of influence by Christian friends. It follows that those of us who are willing to speak a word for Christ have the possibility of becoming meaning-makers in the lives of others.

That's not the full story, of course. If what we say is not authenticated by lives that are being continuously transformed, then we can talk till the proverbial 'cows come home' and it will have little impact. As Don Posterski has wisely written, 'the world needs to see what the Christian life looks like'.[3] People don't need just to listen, they need to look; at the same time they probably won't get there by just looking, they will need someone to talk to—someone who will be able to give the reason 'for the hope that is in you'.

There is something else of note, however. Peter talks about giving a *reason*. There is something very fundamental to our understanding here which is very important, not least in the society which we find ourselves caught up in. We are dealing with ultimate consumers, people for whom choice is an idol. Put simply, it is unlikely that today's consumers will make any life-changing decisions without someone making it very clear why they should want to do that. They will need to be given reasons.

This book is written from the perspective that in speaking to our friends about Christ the Bible's witness is crucial. It is not a mandate for the kind of Bible-bashing that the world fears so much (and rightly so). Neither is it a full-blown treatise on apologetics. Rather, it is an attempt to help Christians who would like to get started on 'giving the reason for the hope you have', to contribute over the dinner table or the coffee break at work, whenever there is a genuine opportunity to add a little 'salt' to the conversation.

The method I have employed is to take a small piece of scripture to which I have added a short application, which hopefully relates to the world we live in today. I pray that what is written will be memorable to you and will help you to give your friends and acquaintances something to think about.

I can promise you that if you take up the challenge to 'salt' a few conversations you will wonder why you didn't start sooner. This book is to encourage you to 'have a go for God'. It is not in any way an attempt to motivate you by making you feel guilty because you have not been doing so to date. Neither is it a 'method' of evangelism. All it assumes is that you have a faith, a Bible, and a tongue. As you read on I suggest you ask the Holy Spirit to give you the courage and motivation to take up this exciting and vital challenge.

1

SETTING THE STAGE

Why is it so hard?

Before looking closer at some Bible passages it is important to reflect upon one or two points. Speaking a word of witness is not something that comes naturally to most of us. Social ethics dictate that one does not get involved in discussion of politics or religion. Moreover, many of us are frightened that if we did start to speak for Christ, then we might quickly get out of our depth and end up drowning! The outcome is that we tend to keep quiet and the tidal wave of secularism continues to swamp all in its path.

What will it take for us to 'get the Good News on to our lips'? I suspect that there are some things that we first need to come to terms with.

Probably a large number of us don't want to speak a word in case our personal reputation suffers. No one wants to be thought of as a religious fanatic! When you stop to think about it, however, fanaticism is mostly a question of the 'tone' and 'volume' of what is being said rather than the content. If we are aggressive or arrogant; if we show an unpreparedness to listen to other people; if we are over-intense and unreasonably dogmatic in our approach, then the majority of people will react to our style alone and never hear what is actually being said.

An important gospel principle is that what is worth having usually bears a cost. Ultimately our starting point is the cross upon which Jesus was cruelly killed. Only when I ponder on the costly nature of his love for me, can I begin to come to grips with his claim upon my life. It is because of his commitment to the human race that he can consistently ask questions about my response, or lack of it.

Jesus once said: 'Those who are ashamed of me and of my words in this adulterous and sinful generation, of them the Son of Man will be ashamed when he comes in the glory of his Father with the holy angels.'[1] This is a sobering and challenging thought! The starting point will be for us to seek God's forgiveness for our silence and ask for the help of his Holy Spirit to give us the courage to 'have a go'.

Much has been written about the Church in recent years. A great deal has been set down about the Church in its 'gathered mode', that is when it comes together for worship, house groups and other church meetings of various kinds. Less attention has been paid to the Church in its other mode—the 'dispersed mode', that is the Church as it manifests itself when it is not meeting together, for example Christians in school, college, their place of work and so on.

Ruth Etchells, writing about the ministry of the laity, highlights this fact: 'We have on the whole, with many honourable and impressive exceptions, put our energy and love into building up the local fellowship and developing its worship, rather than being seized corporately with so passionate a love for the world in which we are set, the world Christ himself loved even to death and beyond, that nothing matters more to us than that Christ might be known to it.'[2]

The sooner we understand that we all have a part to play in all this, the better. There needs to be, however, a great change within most of our churches. A change in all of us—an awareness that we are as much the Church when we are in the world as we are when we gather for church activities.

Why then should I take seriously this matter of speaking a word for Christ?

The Master's mandate
The first reason is that the risen Christ has asked us to. Reflect on these scriptures for a moment:

'Go therefore and make disciples of all nations [literally 'all cultures'], baptizing them in the name of the Father and of the Son and of the Holy Spirit, and teaching them to obey everything that I have commanded you.'[3]

'Peace be with you. As the Father has sent me, so I send you.'[4]

'You will receive power when the Holy Spirit has come upon you; and you will be my witnesses in Jerusalem, in all Judea and Samaria, and to the ends of the earth.'[5]

In all these passages the words come from the lips of the risen Christ. It is important for us to recall that as Christians we have a very strong mandate to share our faith with others.

Clearly within the life of the early Church the Christian community understood this mandate only too well. In Acts Chapter 8 we are told that a persecution broke out against the Church in Jerusalem. The opening verses of this amazing chapter tell us about a number of happenings. First, all the believers, *except the apostles*, were scattered. Secondly, the other believers left Jerusalem and proclaimed the word wherever they went. Thirdly, the Church of God began to take root outside Jerusalem. Why? Because *ordinary* Christian believers were prepared to take some responsibility for sharing the Good News about Jesus.

Approaching it from another angle, it's very interesting to note that when Christianity began to run into persecution, as recorded in Acts Chapter 4, the local authorities took an interesting strategy decision. When they arrested Peter and John, their primary concern was to put an end to the growth of Christianity in Jerusalem. How did they decide to go about that? Acts 4:18 tells us that the Ruling Council called them in and 'ordered them not to speak or teach at all in the name of Jesus'. They clearly felt that the most effective way to stop the Church from spreading *was to stop it from speaking!*

After Peter and John were released by the Council they returned to the Christian community and held a prayer meeting (not an outreach committee!). Again the Spirit came upon them and they 'spoke the word of God with boldness'.[6]

Arrested development

When as Christians we decide to keep quiet about our faith the local church is put under severe pressure. There are a lot of churches in our land with a distorted age profile. This is a polite way of saying that their membership is all too often extremely elderly! Without new members it is not too difficult to work out that the Church is going to have a struggle on its hands in the future.

A friend of mine knew of a woman who, when she became a Christian, was heard to exclaim in the euphoria of her newly found faith that, as far as she could see, 'Jesus was the Church's best kept secret'. Until we get his name on our lips, I fear she may well be right!

Investing in eternity

At one level the achievements of humanity are impressive. Some choose to pursue lucrative careers; others give their minds to creative activity—developing new ideas and inventions, writing great literature or producing acclaimed works of art. So much of what is achieved is, however, no more than transient and we fear that when we leave this mortal life much of what we have contributed will die with us.

Speaking for our faith is one way that we can make an investment for eternity. So many of us have overlooked the hard reality of the Bible's teaching at this point. The prognosis for unbelievers is at best uncertain. Whilst Christians have so often taken the somewhat soft option of believing that eventually all will find a place in heaven (a doctrine called universalism), the Bible is less certain.[7] When the Philippian jailer asked the question, 'What must I do to be saved?', Paul and Silas didn't reply 'Don't worry about it!' Their advice was a little more directive than that: 'Believe on the Lord Jesus, and you will be saved, you and your household.'[8]

Again, the apostle Paul, writing to the Christian community in Ephesus, reminded them that 'it is by grace that you have been saved, through faith—and this is not your own doing, it is the gift of God'.[9] Or again, he spelt out the bottom line to the Christian community in Rome: 'the wages of sin is death, but the free gift of God is eternal life in Christ Jesus our Lord'.[10] Much of what is wrong in today's Church has at its root either an over-optimistic view of human nature or an over-pessimistic view of the power of God.

Trusting Christ is not just a 'nice thing to do' for those who are of a religious disposition. It is a matter of eternal destiny. Until we understand this message, most Christians will treat faith-sharing as a very optional extra. Playing your part in trying to bring your friends to Christ is the best way I know of investing for eternity. What's more, it's exciting!

A platform for personal growth

Often we seem to be caught up in a false dichotomy. On the one hand there are those who will say 'the Church exists primarily for worship', whilst on the other hand others will put mission at the top of the priority list, as if these were mutually conflicting. The dichotomy is brought out when some talk of the Church needing to be 'built up', whilst others stress the need to be 'going out'. While we see the two needs as exclusive goals, we shall probably never do justice to either.

Some years ago the preacher and author, David Watson, made a similar point:

There are two main Hebrew words for worship. The first is hishahawah, which literally means 'a bowing down', a prostration before God, as a sign of profound respect and humility... The second Hebrew word for worship is abodah meaning 'service'. This true worship involves not only praising God with our lips, but also serving him with our lives.[11]

The point is that our worship should in part equip us for service. Most modern liturgies for the service of Holy Communion end with the words of dismissal: 'Go in peace to love and serve the Lord.' But also, lives of service should enrich our sense of all that God has done and is doing for us and thus have a profound impact on our worship.

I know of no more encouraging and energizing experience as a Christian than playing a part in helping family, friends and acquaintances find a faith in Jesus Christ. When you put yourself in the front line it is both demanding and exciting. Just as the performance of a piano recital in public will tell you something about the pianist's preparation, or lack of it, so when we step into the front line for God our own spirituality will be tested. Encouraged to speak for Jesus, you will quickly recognize the need to give proper time and priority to your own spiritual formation. Indeed, you will discover the necessity for that in a new way.

A number of Christians battle on with their attempts to cultivate a fertile spiritual life motivated only by the fact that *not* to try would give them a feeling of guilt. Once you have made the decision to speak for God, you will discover a new motivation for this, and once you do, you will start to grow as a Christian in a way that you have probably not experienced before.

I wonder if you have ever stopped to think about your own Christian faith in this particular way? Surely it is partly true that the reason Christianity has stood the test of time is that our Christian forebears were prepared, in their different ways, to 'speak a word for Christ'. Some of them spoke in the face of torture and death; some, less dramatically, through faithful word and deed added 'salt' to the society in which they found themselves. Between them they kept the light burning brightly. Is it not our responsibility to do the same?

2

A REASON TO BELIEVE?

Fools say in their hearts, 'There is no God.' They are
corrupt, they do abominable deeds; there is no one who
does good.

Psalm 14:1

It was always argued that modern, sophisticated human beings living in the
late twentieth century would never get to grips with the Church's tradi-
tional message. Indeed, the liberal case for Christianity was founded around
the excellent question, 'How could the Gospel be made relevant to contemporary human beings?' This is certainly a very good question and needs
to be constantly asked. The answer, however, was less than helpful, for it
demanded the rewriting of the Jesus story in an attempt to rid it of those
elements thought to be offensive to twentieth-century thinking.
Consequently, the contemporary, 'edited', version was largely denuded of
any supernatural content. Gone were the miracles of Jesus; gone was the
idea that he might have foreseen what was to happen to him; and the idea
of a bodily resurrection was considered positively quaint.

What is, nevertheless, clear as the second millennium AD draws to a
close, is that contemporary and sophisticated humanity is extremely preoccupied with ideas that are comparatively primitive! Only last weekend, as
part of a series on the ancient Chinese philosophy of Feng Shui, a colour
supplement ran an article which suggested that our health, wealth and happiness are affected by the way in which we position our possessions around
the house. The article even recommended that some household objects be
avoided altogether. Bunk beds were thought to be unhelpful as, 'the child
in the bottom bunk is cramped and the child in the top bunk becomes more
insecure'.[1] The present preoccupation with astrology, spiritualism and New
Age practices indicates a prevailing trend. Madam Vasso's recently published biography of the Duchess of York, revealing the Duchess's reliance
on the reading of tarot cards to order her life, is a poignant illustration of

the interface between sophistication and superstition.[2]

Despite the wonder of scientific and technological progress, it would seem that humanity wants to believe that there is more to life than can simply (or not so simply) be explained by scientists. In no way should this be seen as disparaging of today's scientists and technologists, whose achievements are, indeed, quite staggering. It is becoming more and more evident, however, that people need to allow space in their thinking and believing for non-scientific explanations. One of the realities that we Christians have to recognize is that the majority of people will not see Christianity as their first port of call when looking for such explanations. Ironically, it is the very fact that Christians have generally been seen to jettison the supernatural elements of their faith that is responsible for this. It is certainly true that much of the little growth there has been in the Western Church in recent years has taken place in churches that do place emphasis on the supernatural aspects of the Christian faith.

It could be argued that when we exhibit a need to believe in something, we are in danger of believing anything. Bertrand Russell, no great friend of the Christian faith, wrote, 'Man is a credulous animal, and must believe *something*; in the absence of good grounds for belief, he will be satisfied with bad ones.'[3] There is a very real sense in which Russell is right in his thinking. He highlights two important truths. First, that we humans do need to believe in something. Even to claim to believe in nothing is actually a belief! Second, he states that *what* we believe in is important. Russell's point is that what we believe in must have a firm intellectual basis.

There are those today who would be prepared to argue that it doesn't matter what we believe in (within reason), as long as we are firmly committed to that belief. But is that kind of thinking just too simple? For surely, what we believe affects the way we behave? In that sense, what we believe is fundamental.

Nowadays we are a little less upfront than the psalmist of old who affirmed that, 'Fools say in their hearts, "There is no God."'[4] What is striking is that the psalmist immediately makes a connection between belief and behaviour. He continues, 'They are corrupt, they do abominable deeds; there is no one who does good.'

For the psalmist, the behaviour is related to the belief. In his view, the kind of behaviour that ensues is an indication of the belief held. The problem with many beliefs is that they can lead to essentially self-centred behaviour. To adopt an astrological view of life is basically motivated by the attempt to discover about *my* future, *my* chances and what life might look like for *me* and for *my* family. Of course, there are self-centred Christians also. However, I don't think that such people could draw upon their Christianity to defend their self-centredness.

There are naturally many occasions when Christians do 'step out of line' in the way they behave, and over the years we have seen some extraordinary public examples of this. But at the same time, it is also held that Christian values have heavily influenced the cultural foundation of our nation, with its reasonable record on issues such as human rights, lack of corruption in public life and the administration of justice. There may well be room for improvement, but, on the whole, such foundations have served us well.

It was Jesus himself who placed significance both on belief[5] and the importance of lives that offer tangible evidence of such belief. 'No good tree bears bad fruit, nor again does a bad tree bear good fruit; for each tree is known by its own fruit.'[6] The world is initially much more interested in the kind of lives we lead and the kind of qualities we offer, than the intricacies of what we believe. Most people would be extremely hard-pushed to name a professional theologian, but the majority have heard of Mother Teresa of Calcutta and her sacrificial ministry! To say that, however, is certainly *not* to imply that theology, the study of what we believe, is unimportant. Mother Teresa does what she does because of what she believes, namely, that God is a God of love who asks his people to reflect something of his love in the world. Without that inspiration, I believe she would have found it almost impossible to sustain her commitment to her work in giving dignity back to the poor and dying on the streets of Calcutta.

The challenge to us Christians is to become part of the solution and not part of the problem. We can become for some a 'reason' to believe, or we can become a stumbling block to belief. Instead of pointing people to God we can, often inadvertently, point them in the opposite direction. The psalmist was correct, and not a little assertive, in his contention that, 'Fools say in their hearts, "There is no God."' It is an even bigger fool, however, who publicly claims a belief in God and then behaves in a way that gives no credibility to that belief.

We all make mistakes. None of us is perfect. As a street preacher reminded me some years ago, 'If the Church were perfect, you would only spoil it if you joined!' The fact is, however, that if we claim to believe in God, we will need to demonstrate some tangible and visible evidence of this in our lives.

There are many good grounds for our faith. The fact that it has stood the test of time, intellectual attack, persecution and some serious errors of judgment, is sound evidence in itself. The sense of order in the created world and the evidence of the Bible are other important parts of the case for belief. But those of us who own the name of Christ can ourselves be compelling evidence to those around us. For many, we shall be the first piece of evidence that they will closely scrutinize.

3

STRENGTH TO GO ON

Lead us not into temptation.

Luke 11:4 (NIV)

Do you ever feel frustrated by the way you are? If your answer to that question is in the affirmative, then you're in good company. Even St Paul found himself expressing annoyance at his inability to be the person he wanted to be. He once wrote, 'For I know that nothing good dwells within me... I can will what is right, but I cannot do it. For I do not do the good I want, but the evil I do not want is what I do.'[1] Many of us share this frustration within ourselves.

Every year people try a little self-help behaviour modification in the form of New Year's resolutions. We think that the imposition of a little self-discipline will be a good thing. The trouble is we forget it's also a very hard thing. That is why come mid-January most of us have run out of steam and are back to square one!

At one level we cope well with this. We reckon that we might consistently fail, but there are plenty more who are exactly as we are, if not worse. That may well be true, but it's not really the point. Doing things we don't want to do is mostly a negative thing, not least if we are succumbing to destructive impulses within ourselves. You have only got to observe the immense difficulty some people have in giving up smoking to see this at work.

In relationships the ability to make behavioural adjustments is vital, but it is hard. We may firmly intend to give up losing our tempers, but actually doing it is another thing. We may want to stop flirting with members of the opposite sex or desist from driving a car like someone possessed, but where might we make a start? The constant reality of our failure in this area ultimately results in the undermining of our morale and in the end we can both feel and seem beaten people.

A lot of people are a little intimidated by the idea of religion because they feel they could never be good enough. The very idea of 'church' culture with its 'whiter than white' image is immediately alienating to them. Their anxiety is that they will never make the grade and therefore the idea of even trying is too much. I have to say that if I thought that the Christian faith was principally about trying my best within the parameters of my own feeble efforts, I would have given up years ago.

Is there a way we might cope with temptation, or are we simply at the mercy of our own selfish and dark desires? Sometimes reading a newspaper would reluctantly force us to agree with such a pessimistic diagnosis. Maybe even the testimony of our own lives would lead us to a similarly depressing conclusion. There are many of us Christians who find ourselves tripping up time and time again over the same things with the net result that we find ourselves 'clocking in' with God to ask for repeated forgiveness for similar misdemeanours.

In 1 John 1 the writer gives us a clue: 'If we confess our sins, he who is faithful and just will forgive us our sins and cleanse us from all unrighteousness.'[2] It occurs to me that our desire is to be forgiven, but do we really want to be cleansed from our unrighteousness? The problem with sin is that it is ultimately appealing to us. If it were not so we would have no problem avoiding it and the subject of temptation would be an irrelevance.

Most of us when we do wrong feel it in our conscience. H.L. Mencken in his book, *Little Book in C Major*, put it concisely when he defined conscience as 'the inner voice which warns us that someone may be looking'. In the face of our wrongdoing we all want to be forgiven because we feel bad. But do we want to be cleansed of the desire to do wrong?

A story is told of a small boy who was going to church with his mother one morning. He was dressed in his best clothes and was playing in the garden prior to departure. Unfortunately he took a tumble and ended up face down in a very muddy puddle. His previous smart apparel was covered in mud. His mother was not pleased to see her son in this state. Indeed, she was very angry and was just about to administer a punishment when the boy looked at her with large, pleading eyes. His mother was won over. She dismissed him with these words: 'All right, I'll forgive you this time. Go upstairs and get in the bath quickly or we'll be late for church.' Immediately the boy protested, 'I don't want a bath, I don't need a bath!' We all want to be forgiven, but do we want to be cleansed?

The Bible gives us help with the business of dealing with temptation.

The Lord's Prayer given to us by Jesus himself invites us to pray regularly that we shall be delivered from temptation. It is good to remind ourselves that prayer is a great resource in this matter. Prayer enables us to ask God to send the power of the Holy Spirit to help us at such times.

I used to read the story of the temptations of Jesus[3] and wonder that after forty days in the desert with God, Jesus could summon the strength to repudiate the subtleties of the devil. After Jesus had fasted forty days the devil's first tack was to tempt him into utilizing his power to turn stones into bread. Knowing how jumpy I get after missing one meal I marvelled that Jesus could resist! I now believe that my reading of this story was misguided. The assumption I made was that Jesus was at his weakest having been in the desert for so long. I now see that actually the opposite is likely to be true. After forty days of prayer and fasting Jesus was at his *strongest* in terms of standing firm in the face of temptation. Similarly, our ability to resist temptation will be strengthened by learning to be prayerful people.

One thing these temptation stories make clear is Jesus' reliance upon scripture in the face of temptation. Each of the three times that Jesus was tempted he confronted the devil with scripture—though the story also indicates that the devil is not beyond quoting some himself! It is unlikely that the use of scripture in this sense is mystical. It is not the mere reciting of the Bible that wards off temptation. It is knowing the Bible well enough to know what God's word is in given situations and trusting that word. Over the years many people, sometimes Christians, have sought to avoid the implications of God's word, wondering whether or not their particular situation might be an exception to the general rule. Twenty years of pastoral ministry have made it clear to me that people who go their own way are never ultimately blessed by doing so.

The writer of the Epistle to the Hebrews puts another 'spin' on all this. He speaks of Jesus' identification with our temptations, but significantly also his ability to overcome them. Speaking of Jesus, he wrote these words: 'For we do not have a high priest who is unable to sympathize with our weaknesses, but we have one who in every respect has been tested as we are, yet without sin.' Because of this the writer continues, 'Let us therefore approach the throne of grace with boldness, so that we may receive mercy and find grace to help in time of need.'[4]

The assumption made in the New Testament is this—that we *shall* be tempted. The question is 'when' rather than 'if'. The problem is, how shall we deal with it? The difficult part for us is that succumbing to temptation always appears to have some kind of benefit. Giving in to selfish desires such as gluttony or lust or smoking or drinking, promises us the 'gain' of short-term pleasure. When saints of old were tempted by the State to renounce their Christian faith or die, the temptation must have been huge. Invariably the long-term view of giving in is less promising.

A final point. A soul friend can play an important part in helping us stand firm. Someone to whom we voluntarily offer a measure of account-ability can be an invaluable source of strength. There is a dimension to all this that can only properly be dealt with through such 'horizontal' relation-ships of accountability. Such people will often give us sound and practical advice. They will encourage us to steer clear of situations in which we might fall; they will help us identify and work on our own personal areas of weakness.

The cause of our personal development will be aided greatly by our will-ingness and ability to know how to deal with temptation. We shall find strength in Christ for ourselves in this matter. How willing are we to help those who do not know him to access that same gentle strength that God wants for us all?

4

SLAYING LIFE'S GIANTS

**David said to Saul, 'Let no one's heart fail because of
him [Goliath]; your servant will go and fight with this
Philistine.'**

1 Samuel 17:32

How big is your God? In the midst of life it is easy to lose a right perspective. Part of our humanity is to tend to deny our problems. When we ask people, 'How are you?', we don't really expect them to tell us. Standing on the doorstep of church, as clergy do, I recall feeling very humbled when, after I asked a woman how she was, she burst into tears and said she was in a real state. Part of me wanted to remind her that she was supposed to say, 'I'm fine, thank you!'

Let's be honest. In the company of Christians it is sometimes hard to admit we have problems. We somehow feel that to acknowledge this would run the risk of our being regarded as 'unspiritual'. Surprisingly, many unchurched[1] individuals are scared of Christians because they fear that they are 'not good enough'; at another level they feel that their lack of 'goodness' will result in their being judged harshly by us.

Yet, as far as I can see, we all have problems. Refusing to admit that we do, or pretending that they are trivial, doesn't mean that they will miraculously disappear. If only it were that simple! When our difficulties, whatever they are, start to get us down we quickly lose a sense of perspective, which has the effect of adding to our depression. In Psalm 73 we see a perfect example of this. Clearly the writer of the psalm has let his problems get him down:

Truly God is good to the upright, to those who are pure in heart.
But as for me, my feet had almost stumbled; my steps had nearly slipped.
For I was envious of the arrogant; I saw the prosperity of the wicked.
For they have no pain; their bodies are sound and sleek.

They are not in trouble as others are; they are not plagued like other people.[2]

Two things are worthy of note. First, the psalmist begins with a nice spiritual platitude, 'Truly God is good to the upright...' That's a constant danger for the people of God: to be inauthentic by pretending that we're OK when we are not. Second, the psalmist has lost his sense of proportion. Though it's his perspective, he's wrong. It is nonsense to suggest that arrogant and wicked people are beyond illness and everyday problems. That is just what he felt at the time.

Authenticity demands that we don't pretend. That is why Jesus gave the Pharisees such a hard time, calling them hypocrites on more than one occasion.[3] Having problems isn't the problem; it's the way we deal with them that counts. For all of us, but especially the unchurched, there is the fundamental question as to whether God *can* actually help us with our problems.

When David stepped up to take on Goliath there must have been a few doubters around; frankly, had I been there at the time, I would have been one of them. David was a boy whose background was farming, not fighting;[4] he played the harp;[5] and at first sight Goliath was not overtly frightened![6] Yet David triumphed, claiming God's help in defeating this monster of a man.[7]

Thinking about this wonderful story is a reminder that the Bible is full of examples of God's people overcoming insurmountable problems. Indeed, the whole of Christian history seems littered with examples of Christian men and women triumphing against impossible odds. Problem-solving is a recognized skill in leadership training today. How much more might we 'solve' our problems by drawing on the resources of Almighty God? David's confidence in God's strength is what stands out in the story of his encounter with Goliath.

When Jesus says in Mark's Gospel, 'Have faith in God. Truly I tell you, if you say to this mountain, "Be taken up and thrown into the sea," and if you do not doubt in your heart, but believe that what you say will come to pass, it will be done for you'[8] he does not mean, of course, that he wants to empower us to make cosmetic changes to the universe! I think what he means is that our faith could assist us in dealing with the mountains in our lives. For most of us that will not be an easy truth to assimilate.

David's faith was outstanding. In the face of the giant he confidently predicted that God would deal with Goliath. I imagine there were large numbers of David's fellow Israelites who were embarrassed by David's seemingly naïve confidence, fearing that when Goliath laid David out, not only would that be one less Israelite, it would also allow Goliath to mock God. Yet David triumphed over Goliath, who had previously posed a huge military problem to the Israelites. What was it in David's approach that made the difference?

The first thing was that David both saw and owned the problem. The story tells us that David was undertaking a logistical task in supplying his brothers, who were in the front line of the battle, with provisions. In other words, his principle reason for being there was not military. It was when David saw Goliath step out on to the battlefield that he saw the size of the problem! Even more, he saw his fellow Israelites' response to the problem: 'All the Israelites, when they saw the man, fled from him and were very much afraid.'[9] The impact of a problem has much to do with our reaction to it. Despite the king's attractive offer of financial inducement, no one wanted to 'have a go' with Goliath. While everyone else ran for cover, David stood and squarely faced the problem.

The second thing was that David appeared to be focused not upon the size of the problem, but rather on the size of his God. It is curious that at such times in our lives it seems easier to focus on our problem rather than of our God. I sense this fact is important. Like David's fellow Israelites our inclination when facing life's mountains is to run away. The reason for this is obvious. We know that in our own strength we shall fail—though it doesn't stop us from trying most of the time.

Finally, David overcame the problem. Against all the odds and the expectations of his colleagues, David slew the giant. Too many of us take one look at the giants in our lives and run away. Alternatively we ignore them in the hope that they might go away. David shows us that problem-solving is potentially turbocharged when we bring God into the picture. How big is your God?

5

THE GOD WHO GUIDES

You guide me with your counsel, and afterward you will receive me with honour.

Psalm 73:24

There's a delightful story about a man who was attending a silent retreat for the very first time. After the first couple of days he was feeling bored stiff and yearned to get back into the 'real world', even if only for a short while. So, having thought up a means of 'escape', he was sneaking out through a side door of the monastery, just before lunch, when he unfortunately bumped into the abbot. The abbot, a rather austere character, asked him in a sombre tone where he was going. Seeking to justify his departure, on the spur of the moment the man replied, 'The Lord has shown me that I have to get down to the local shops', whereupon the abbot fixed the man with a forbidding stare and declared, 'Clearly the Lord has not also shown you that today is early closing!'

The question of how God guides us is not at all simple. Although I have already discovered it for myself, a good many fellow Christians also tell me that this matter is extremely complex. We should certainly think carefully before prefixing our own ideas with phrases such as, 'The Lord has shown me...', otherwise in treating the subject so superficially we could well give the impression to those who hear us that we are joking with the name of God. Whether or not we really want our will or God's will to be done in our lives is something we do not always find easy to discern.

There are many issues that I sense God is happy for us to sort out on our own. What we should have for lunch tomorrow or where to look for a car parking space, for example, are not matters that I believe Christians, or indeed anyone else, should spend too much time worrying about. At the same time, however, we know that we have decisions to make where God's wisdom would be extremely welcome and necessary. Life's larger issues are very important—to God and to me! What kind of career to take up, whether to marry, whom to marry, where to live, what manner of lifestyle to adopt, are just some of the important questions where the 'right' or 'wrong' decision will significantly affect not only the course of our own lives but that of others around us also.

The other point to make by way of introduction is that it may be helpful to distinguish between what I will call general guidance and individual guidance. By general guidance I mean that part of God's will that is intended for the lives of all God's people, rather than to specific individuals alone. We can see that in the Bible God gives guidance for how he wants all his people to live their lives. In this sense his guidance is for all. For example, when God reveals that adultery, theft, lying and blasphemy are wrong, he intends *all* his people to regard such things as 'out of court'. This kind of general guidance is to help us to get the most out of life as we try to live according to God's rules. Discovering what God wants in this respect is in many ways not very difficult, but it is attempting to follow that guidance that can often be extremely hard.

Individual guidance is even more complex. It is seeking to discern those issues that relate specifically to our personal lives, or knowing what God wants in the life of the family we may be part of. This can be much more difficult to discern and worries some people greatly. The stakes often seem incredibly high. As I have already said, if we make a mistake with a career change, or choose the wrong marriage partner, lives other than our own could also be wrecked. I have seen Christians head off in a particular direction convinced that they were doing so as a response to God's leading, only to end up in a real mess. Did they fail to understand God's guidance in the first place, or was it rightly understood with God's intention being that they should be led into experiencing certain difficulties? These are undoubtedly questions that people can be left asking.

Paul, in Romans, writes of a deeply reassuring safety net which it is good for us to remember: 'We know that all things work together for good for those who love God, who are called according to his purpose.'[1] Just as an earthly parent will need to know when to be directive in guidance and when to allow a child to discover things on its own, so our heavenly Father's relationship with us is conditioned principally by love. When our own children decide to ignore our example or our advice, we don't stop caring about the outcome in their lives. We try to help them learn from their experience. So God doesn't stop loving us even when we make a mistake.

He helps us to recover and to learn from the experience.

The purpose of this chapter in the light of the previous chapter is to look a little more specifically at how we might access God's guidance. What resources are there available to help us discern God's will in our lives? I believe there are five things we need to think about.

1. The Bible

The Bible is a really important tool in this matter of discerning God's will, both generally and individually. The psalmist wrote, 'Your word is a lamp to my feet and a light to my path.'[2] The role of the Bible in offering general guidance to all God's people is relatively straightforward. In reading the Bible regularly and studying it together with God's people, we learn what values and standards God requires of us. In this sense the Bible offers us a real challenge as we seek to ask the Holy Spirit to enable us to become more like Jesus.

On occasions the Bible can give us individual guidance. This doesn't mean closing our eyes, thumbing through the pages of scripture and sticking a pin in the page in order that we might 'be given a verse'. That said, it is amazing how when we read the scriptures regularly our daily reading offers an insight on a particular area of guidance we have been wrestling with. We should always be trying to relate the Bible to our lives. The more we read and study the Bible together, the more we can become adept at hearing God speak to us through its pages.

2. Prayer

Prayer is a tremendous gift from God which enables us to seek his will for us. Every time we pray the Lord's Prayer we express a commitment to prioritize what God wants in our lives, over and above our own agenda: 'Our Father... your will be done on earth as it is in heaven.' There is a trap to be avoided here. Don't think that prayer is only about talking to God, or even worse talking at him! It is vitally important that we learn the art of listening to God. The value of training ourselves to allow space for silence in our prayer life is one of the most significant discoveries we can make, but because of our activist culture it will come neither easily nor readily to most of us. It will require hard work on our part.

In his letter to the Colossians, Paul speaks of something that is important for us to remember in discerning the will of God in prayer. He urges the Colossian Christians, 'Let the peace of Christ rule in your hearts.'[3] Literally, the Greek text means, 'Let the peace of Christ be the umpire.' The idea here is that we should not proceed with a major change of direction unless we have a sense of peace about doing so. This may be something you have already experienced in yourself. It is even possible for us, at one level, to feel we would prefer not to follow a certain course of action, and yet still have a sense of peace about it. The problem is that many of us have developed such frenzied lifestyles that we do not find it easy to give ourselves the time to find God's peace within us over a particular issue.

Isaiah delivered a message from God to his people: 'in quietness and in trust shall be your strength'.[4] It is doubtful whether God would change his message for today's Church.

3. Christian friends
One of the great blessings of the Church is being part of a Christian family within which we can test out God's will. It is a very positive thing to have others with whom we can try to discover what God is saying to us. When Peter and John were forbidden by the Council in Jerusalem from speaking in the name of Jesus, they immediately went back to the Christian congregation there and prayed about it together. Their conclusion was that they had little choice but to continue to speak the word of God with boldness.[5]

Many of us have had occasion to be extremely thankful for the advice and counsel of other Christians. Sometimes it is especially helpful to think through a particular course of action with Christians of greater maturity than ourselves. There are probably very few important decisions we make that we ought not to check out with others. A possible catch here, however, is that we sometimes know people well enough to anticipate what they are likely to say in a given situation.

In 2 Chronicles, Chapter 18, the half-amusing story is told of Ahab, King of Israel, consulting his own group of paid prophets as to whether or not he should go to Ramoth-Gilead and fight. The said prophets were unanimous, if not histrionic, in encouraging him to do so and promised him certain victory. The King of Judah, Jehosophat, who was present at Ahab's court, asked whether there were any other prophets around who could be consulted. Ahab told him of the prophet, Micaiah, but added, 'I hate him, for he never prophesies anything favourable about me, but only disaster.'[6]

Micaiah was consulted. At first he colluded with the paid prophets' assertion that the king would go to Ramoth-Gilead and win. When questioned further, however, Micaiah prophesied a scene of desolation and defeat for the kingdoms of Israel and Judah, foreseeing also the death of Ahab. His words were truth, for a dreadful defeat took place. Chapter 18 ends with the pathetic and mortally wounded Ahab propped up in his chariot, where he died at sunset.

The message is clear. Don't just go to those who will tell you what you want to hear. Go to those who love you enough to tell you the truth. It is better to be given the truth than an empty ratification of what you want to do.

4. Open doors and closed doors

At times when a course of action is not clear to us we can, as we say, 'push open a few doors'. This means starting out on a course of action to see if it gathers any momentum and if the next 'door' (that is, an opportunity to progress the action) opens for us, we will trust that it is God who has opened it and therefore carry on. Equally, when a 'door' closes we accept that this is not the direction that God wishes us to take.

The Acts of the Apostles gives examples of this. In Chapter 16 we are told that Paul and Timothy, having passed through Phrygia and Galatia, were 'forbidden by the holy Spirit to speak the word in Asia'.[7] We are not told how the Spirit made that clear. What is obvious is that this was a door that somehow was closed to them. On the other hand, in Acts Chapter 8, Philip responded to some kind of angelic prompting to go and stand on the road between Jerusalem and Gaza. A door was opened, and Philip by the 'close of business' had baptized a eunuch from Ethiopia![8]

5. Close encounters...

God sometimes uses extraordinary and supernatural ways to guide his people. It has been noted that probably God's rationale for this manner of guidance is when all else fails. Such guidance would include visions or dreams. A major shift in the early Church's understanding was brought about by a vision that the apostle Peter saw.[9] Paul, on occasions, was guided by visions.[10]

I don't myself believe that this is necessarily the primary way in which God guides his people. But it is a way that God clearly uses on occasions. There are some Christians who appear to believe that this is God's favoured way of leading his people, but the case is not convincing. On the other hand, there are others who feel that God never guides in this way and who are, therefore, unreasonably sceptical.

It is worth noting that these 'strands' of guidance are not mutually exclusive of each other. Indeed, it is quite the opposite. I was told of the navigational problems faced when entering one of the Mediterranean ports. The secret of success was to steer the ship in such a way that it lined up with a set of navigational lights. Once this had been done the sailor could set course and enter the harbour safely. The analogy is obvious: the more of these strands of guidance we can line up, the better.

Jesus made it clear that the matter of doing God's will is of fundamental importance. He once said to his disciples, 'Not everyone who says to me "Lord, Lord" will enter the kingdom of heaven, but only the one who does the will of my Father in heaven.'[11] The assumption which underlies carrying out God's will is knowing it. The fact that God guides his people is a real encouragement in a society where choice is perceived as a virtue.

When my family and I visited the Alhambra Palace in southern Spain we initially attempted to find our way around the beautiful rooms with the help of the official guidebook. After a short while we realized it was almost impossible to read the small print of the book and at the same to take in and enjoy all the beauty of the place. The visit was greatly enriched when we suddenly found ourselves tagging on to a guided tour. To travel with a guide is always more satisfactory.

I sense that as we journey through life we shall benefit from the guidance of Jesus who longs to travel with us. Those to whom Jesus is a stranger need to know that he can become both a friend and a guide. He's just an invitation away.

6

THE LORD'S MY SHEPHERD—1

The Lord is my shepherd, I shall not want.

Psalm 23:1

The Bible attributes this psalm to David. Here was a man who, like most of us, had some shade as well as some bright light in his life. The young man who victoriously killed the Philistine's answer to a heavyweight boxing champion, Goliath,[1] was the same man who committed adultery with another man's wife and then arranged for her husband to be lost in battle.[2] Although we tend to exalt biblical heroes like David to superstar status, he was in fact an ordinary person who faced the same temptations and failures that we experience. His place in Christian history is because at key times in his life he trusted God with an unswerving trust, and in consequence his ordinariness became extraordinary. One of the most defeatist statements I can ever make as a Christian is, 'I could never be like that.' If that is our starting point, we will never know!

The bottom line is this. David had reached a point in his life when he could make this extraordinary assertion: 'The Lord is my shepherd, I shall not want.' It seems to be the comment of a man who had reviewed where fulfilment and security in life might be found. He had concluded, with many great people throughout the period of Christian history, that it is found supremely through faith in God.

The question for us today is whether the faith that brought David to his confident assertion could do the same for us. Could the implicit security of David's statement become ours? These are crucial questions for people like us and, in particular, for the hundreds of thousands of people who claim to believe in God, but aren't really sure what that means in terms of their daily living. 'The Lord is my shepherd, I shall not want.' The affirmation David makes feels like a safe place to be.

In one way it is not surprising in our materialist, lottery-obsessed age that many people do not like to admit to their desperation for more. Most people prefer to pretend that these things don't really matter to them. A common feature of dependency illnesses is denial of the problem! However, a cursory look at society's behaviour reveals the harsh truth. The weekly queues for lottery tickets, the quest for constantly upgrading what we have, the frantic Christmas shopping scenario are all signs of a society obsessed with materialism.

It has to be said that there *is* a measure of security to be had from material things. To have nothing does not necessarily make us feel secure either. Jesus said, 'One does not live by bread alone',[3] but he did not suggest that we could live without bread! The real question is 'Where does my security lie?' It is possible to be extremely rich and extremely insecure. It is also possible to be poor and to know real security. How can this be?

Think for a moment about the building process. The strength of a building is in no small measure related to the strength of its foundations. Recently one of the clergy houses for which I am responsible has begun to move alarmingly; large cracks are appearing all over it. The structural engineer makes it clear in his report that, given the local geology, the foundations were never adequate enough to cope. The result is an insecure building, which if left alone will ultimately collapse. When you build it is better to build upon a firm foundation.

The same is true in the building process of life. It is better to build upon a firm foundation. When God created us he created us with a spiritual aspect to our nature.[4] He made us to exist in relationship with himself. Unless we give some attention to that spiritual side of our nature we will never find real security in life. People need to understand this. To extend the above analogy slightly, it is part of the 'geology' of our human nature. Any foundation that disregards the raw material of a faith in God is in danger of imminent collapse. It explains why it is possible to be very rich and insecure; it also explains why it is possible to have very little and yet know what it is to be secure.

'The Lord is my shepherd, I shall not want.' To be able to join with David in saying this is to discover a truth that will set us up for life. Writing hundreds of years later, St Paul expanded the same theme: 'I have learned to be content with whatever I have. I know what it is to have little, and I know what it is to have plenty. In any and all circumstances I have learned the secret of being well-fed and of going hungry, of having plenty and of being in need. I can do all things through him who strengthens me.'[5]

To those who strive for security built upon the 'deceitfulness of wealth', the message in the first part of this psalm is crucial. You may have noticed that in the Bible God is often likened to a rock. The idea to be conveyed here is that God is immovable and secure. If we trust him, he will not let us down because he is a firm foundation.

A lot of people go through life wanting. They might well want more money or more things. Alternatively, they may have other felt needs. That's all right—it's part of being human. But when my want becomes an obsession it becomes unhealthy and destructive.

David in his earlier life had wanted another man's wife, Bathsheba. His want had become an obsession to the point that he conveniently arranged for her husband to be re-posted to the most dangerous battlefield in the war effort. David learnt his lesson. He came to see that his needs could quickly become obsessive wants. He finally understood that the only way to keep all this in check was to place his life in the hands of God, the Good Shepherd. Only then could he claim the strength from knowing that the best kind of security cannot be bought—it can only be received.

7

THE LORD'S MY SHEPHERD—2

...your rod and staff—they comfort me.

Psalm 23:4

Is it rational to believe in the goodness of God? The implication of David's statement recorded in Psalm 23:1 is that God *is* good and that he can be trusted. That question is one of profound significance. The vast majority of people in our country today claim to hold a belief in God. A recent poll suggested that 50 per cent of the population still believe in the resurrection of Jesus.[1]

But the issue of whether people believe *in* God clouds the issue of what they believe *about* him. The experience of living in a world where so much goes wrong has led many people to conclude that if there is a God he is either to be avoided at all costs, or, at the very least, kept at a very safe distance from everyday living.

The constant suffering and violence that invade our living rooms via the television have undoubtedly left us with some big questions. When Thomas Hamilton walked off the street into the primary school in Dunblane and shot dead fifteen children and their teacher, most of us found it extremely hard to explain *why* God apparently allowed it to happen. Our natural response was rightly to weep rather than to offer trite explanations. If we are being honest, we shall go through seasons in life when our belief in the goodness of God will be severely stretched. One of the greatest Christian apologists of this century, C.S. Lewis, following the death of his wife, wrote graphically about the deep anger and outrage he felt:

What chokes every prayer and every hope is the memory of all the prayers H. and I offered and all the false hopes we had. Not hopes raised merely by our own wishful thinking; hopes encouraged, even forced upon us, by false diagnoses, by X-ray photographs, by strange remissions, by one temporary recovery that might have ranked as a miracle. Step by step we were 'led up the garden path'. Time after time, when He seemed most gracious He was really preparing the next torture.[2]

It would not take a great act of discernment to work out that on the day C.S. Lewis wrote those words he would hardly have echoed David's words in Psalm 23! There are certainly times in our lives when we feel that we are left badly wanting.

If we feel that life is hard, it is only natural that we shall want to know why that is.

This a big question and one that is almost impossible to answer. There may be examples of suffering where a link between cause and effect is evident. For instance, if I suffer from lung cancer having smoked forty cigarettes a day for fifty years, the connection, in the light of contemporary medical knowledge, is clear. But what about those who shared the same habit and did not get lung cancer? Is anything straightforward?

Whatever David meant when he wrote, 'The Lord is my shepherd, I shall not want', he couldn't have meant that he would never find himself in life situations where he felt himself to be in want. I think he meant that ultimately, with God on his side, he would never be without hope; that whatever came his way in life, he would always somehow, somewhere, find the strength to cope.

Detailed intellectual discussions about the reality of human suffering are important, but when it's *my* suffering they tend to go out of the window. In the end I am not helped by conjecture about why suffering happens so much as in need of strength to help me to cope. There are those, of course, who would try to tell me that 'if you give your life to Jesus', then all your problems will be over. It would be comfortable to feel that such a thing were true, but it is surely a corruption of what Christians believe. The life of Jesus and the experience of Christians down the ages render such an oversimplification untenable.

Alan Paton expressed it well in his excellent book *Cry, the Beloved Country* when he wrote: 'I have never thought a Christian would be free from suffering. For our Lord suffered. And I have come to believe that He suffered, not to save us from suffering, but to teach us how to bear suffering. For He knew that there is no life without suffering.'

The pages of Christian history may not bear testimony to endless numbers of men and women who found it easy to give full and conclusive answers as to *why* there is human suffering. Yet those same pages do point to hundreds of thousands of brave men and women who have found the strength to endure terrible suffering with both dignity and courage.

An aspect of Christian belief that we have to a great extent lost touch with at this present time is the promise of eternal life—the belief that for the Christian believer, death is not the end, but a new beginning. When St Paul wrote, 'the wages of sin is death, but the free gift of God is eternal life in Christ Jesus our Lord',[3] he was expressing something fundamental about the beliefs of the early Christians.

In the face of much persecution and suffering, they gained great inspiration from their unshakeable conviction that whatever life threw at them they would ultimately be victorious. They believed that there was a state awaiting them which would be free from suffering and pain and where the injustices they had suffered in this life would be put right. This belief gave them the courage to face suffering and death with great courage and confidence. It didn't mean that the pain they suffered was any less, but it put that pain in a new perspective. They knew where they were going!

It reminds me of the experience many of us have prior to going on holiday—those tense few days before departure when there is too much to be done in too little time. Family members become more and more fractious and irritated by each other in the mad rush to get everything done before leaving. Each year I ask myself the question, 'Is is all worth it?' The answer, a few days later, when we are relaxing in a pleasant environment away from the pressures of everyday living, is a resounding 'YES'. When you know where you are going it makes the hassle of the preparation and journey a little easier to bear. If Christians have any sense of where they are going, then they might be able to place the trials of the journey in a wider perspective.

'The Lord is my shepherd, I shall not want.' If the key question on suffering is not 'Why does it happen?' but 'How shall we cope?', then we shall have a decision to make. When suffering comes will we choose to suffer with God or without him? No prizes for guessing what David's answer would have been!

8

I'LL NOT WANDER

He leads me beside still waters; he restores my soul. He leads me in right paths for his name's sake.

Psalm 23:2–3

Some years ago, before I was ordained, I worked in the world of commerce. I recall an occasion when I made my first visit to London on company business and in a company car. I felt eight feet tall. I arrived there in plenty of time and parked the car at a parking meter, then went to see our clients, determined to impress.

After the meeting I returned to where I thought I had left the company car, only to discover that many of the streets in central London looked identical and that I had lost my bearings. I wandered for hours searching in vain for the car and then had to suffer the humiliation of returning to the clients to ask for their help in tracking it down. Eventually we found it.

People who are wandering are often looking for something. Indeed they are often lost. Many people have that sense of being wanderers on the journey of life. There is in religious writing the idea of life being a pilgrimage. The pilgrim, of course, does know where he is going, but there are many people who are wandering aimlessly.

We need to help people make connections between journey and destination. Life can be more fulfilling when we discover some kind of purpose and direction, and it is precisely because a lot of people lack that sense of direction and experience life as a series of disconnected 'culs-de-sac' that we live in a society which appears to be frustrated and angry. Such frustration and anger quickly erode any sense of responsibility and become more intense when roads which showed such promise turn out to lead nowhere.

What is it that a wanderer needs? The simple answer is that the wanderer needs either a guide or a map, perhaps even both. David, the writer of Psalm 23, knew what it was to wander and at times in his life had found himself badly 'off track', but he came to a point in his life where he could affirm that his life was back on track. 'The Lord is my shepherd'—of that shepherd David could be sure.

David had found that through his faith in God he had discovered the kind of guidance that took him to those places in life where he could discover both nourishment and fulfilment. The Good Shepherd wants to do that for people today.

The Good Shepherd is not only a great guide but also offers an inspirational map—the Bible, which makes available priceless wisdom on how to get the most from life and how to prepare for our final destination. For this journey intelligence is helpful, wisdom is vital. In the Bible God offers us his wisdom for living. As our society today abundantly illustrates, there is much wandering when individuals have lost any sense of travelling with a moral map. They wander from relationship to relationship, from marriage to marriage, from experience to experience, only pausing when their latest attempt becomes habit-forming.

There is, however, a problem in all this with the way we live in twentieth-century society. It is our activism; our busyness. We seem to be a society addicted to the idea that to be busy is good. Indeed, we make people feel as though there is something wrong with their lives if they are not busy—and this contributes to the stigma of being unemployed. The philosopher Descartes is attributed with having said 'I think, therefore I am.'[1] Today he might have felt it appropriate to rephrase that statement into 'I do, therefore I am.'

The downside of our activism is that we leave ourselves little time for personal reflection; little space for just 'being' rather than 'doing'. Such a climate is hostile to religious thought. It makes us short-termist rather than long-termist; focused upon the 'now' rather than the 'what will be'. That is why so many of us have little sense of destination, making the route through life the journey of the wanderer rather than the pilgrim.

There is limited and largely anecdotal evidence that people are tired of society's activism. Retreat houses, places where one can go and create some space for personal reflection and growth, are much in demand. Although this is to be welcomed, these 'gardens of tranquillity' will not be enough to change a society hell-bent on doing.

The tough issue for us as Christians is whether we stand together against the activism of our society or whether we inadvertently collude with it. It occurs to me that many of our churches offer just another form of activism.

A cursory glance at the weekly news-sheet of a large number of churches, especially 'lively' churches, reveals a predictable pattern of activity. Every night of the week there is something for the faithful to do. We must face the painful question of whether or not our churches, whilst they continue to provide another form of activism, will have any cutting edge in today's society.

This Good Shepherd of whom David speaks leads him first to 'still waters'. Those words have a significance which we might all too easily miss. The first break in the journey of today's wandering sheep might need to be at those 'still waters'.

Have we taken a drink from them ourselves?

9

I'LL NOT WORRY

Even though I walk through the darkest valley, I fear no evil; for you are with me...

Psalm 23:4

On a recent trip abroad a friend looked at me across the breakfast table and said, 'I'm worried.' When I quizzed him as to the cause of his anxiety he retorted, 'I'm worried that I can't think of anything to worry about!'

Many of us live in an almost permanent state of worry, and on the face of it there is plenty to worry about. Life has a certain fragility about it. There is a very fine line between life being OK and it being not OK. Events such as the terrible earthquake in Kobe, Japan, or, at another level, the wife or husband who suddenly discovers that their spouse is having an affair, are reminders that we are vulnerable—often to forces and events that are beyond our control. Whenever I hear an ambulance racing from the scene of an accident it reminds me that the person in the back of the vehicle got up that morning very likely thinking that that day would be much the same as the day before. In a microsecond a life is shattered and in consequence a network of the lives of family and friends is also disrupted in an instant.

I sense that deep within us we know that life is fragile and that we human beings, whatever we may deny, have an innate sense that this is so. Those of us who are parents feel that sense acutely, particularly perhaps during those tender moments when we look at our children sleeping in their beds. Their innocence and vulnerability puts us in touch with our own similar feelings.

Our initial response to this fragility is denial. All of us, but men in particular, resist admitting that we are fragile beings. To do so, we think, would be to admit that we have weakness. Indeed, we invent behaviour which we hope will cushion us from the realities of life's fragility.

For some the lure of surrounding ourselves with our material goods is the route we choose. Health insurance and life assurance policies, property, cars, pensions and possessions will, we believe, make us feel more secure. And in a way they do. To not have some insurance behind us is mostly irresponsible. But will all that ultimately shield us from life's fragility? I don't think so. A wealthy friend whose child was very sick rejected the shallowness of financial security. As we looked at his sick child he somewhat despairingly said of all his material wealth, 'All this stuff counts for nothing just now.'

Others make more destructive choices to shield themselves from life and vulnerability. Some will abuse alcohol or drugs in an effort to anaesthetize themselves. Even more perplexing is the fact that some people will even hijack religion to help them escape life's reality. Karl Marx observed that 'religion... is the opium of the people.'[1] In its way it was a shrewd observation. He saw that some people would always use faith as an escape route from life's reality. The tendency of some Christians to construct a version of the Christian faith that is emphatically other-worldly—'pie in the sky when you die'—is both astonishing and unbalanced. To deny responsibility for this world on the basis that there is a better life to come is only part of the picture. Similarly, the 'come to Jesus and all your problems will be over' may score highly on wishful thinking, but is a denial of reality, common sense and biblical witness. When life takes a downturn we need to ask the question 'How will people cope?' This is not to scare them, but to help them prepare for the likely reality that there will be times in their lives when they will face fragility.

In this psalm David makes a claim worthy of close scrutiny: 'Even though I walk through the darkest valley, I fear no evil, for you are with me.'[2] It appears that David is implying two things. Firstly, he accepts that life is a fragile business; he knows there will be days when we walk through the darkest valley. Indeed, David knew some dark times in his own life. But, secondly, he could go on from there and state that life's valleys no longer held any fear for him. Why? Because David asserts 'YOU ARE WITH ME.'

When we speak of God's protection and guidance we are not speaking of a God who occasionally intervenes in our lives at key times. We are talking of a God who wants to travel with us wherever we go. A God who offers us his strength and his presence in our lives. A presence that can make a huge difference.

It's dramatic to see the difference the presence of a parent makes to a child facing an unknown and unnerving experience. It doesn't necessarily lessen the pain, but it helps enormously just to have Mum or Dad nearby. David says something similar as he reflects upon life's fragility. The knowledge that his heavenly Father goes with him into whatever life can throw at him means a very great deal.

Throughout the era of Christian history, individuals have borne witness to this fact. The promise of God's presence makes a difference to living. In good times, but especially in bad times. Whether at the opera or on the operating table; at times of celebration or times of consolation; at the funfair or the funeral parlour, the knowledge of God's presence makes a difference.

The kind of security most people need for life is more likely to be gained from a new perspective rather than just another new policy. Peter, writing in the New Testament to a suffering Christian community, says 'Cast all your anxiety on him, because he cares for you.'[3] Our anxieties and 'cares' can be destructive. They can rob us of our peace and our health. The Good Shepherd calls to each of us. Who will respond to his voice?

10

HE WAS A LITTLE MAN

> He [Zacchaeus] was trying to see who Jesus was, but on
> account of the crowd he could not, because he was short
> in stature.

Luke 19:3

'Small is beautiful' is a phrase that resounds widely today. The loss of the
small village or town shops and their replacement by large supermarkets,
though hard to resist, is lamented by many. The growth of larger units in
both commerce and retailing may be good news for prices, but bad news in
terms of the way it tends towards the process of dehumanization so-called
'developed' civilization seems intent on. Making a complaint (or a com-
mendation) to a large organization feels more like dealing with a system
than with human beings. In all sorts of areas of life we could be easily per-
suaded that small *is* beautiful.

There is, however, a largely notable exception to this generally appealing
slogan. It is the individual. A lot of people who are small would like to be a
little bigger. That said, it is equally true that a good number of people who
are big would like to be a little smaller! But it is not just a physical matter.
It is the fact that most of us don't like to be made to feel small. When we
talk about feeling small, we are talking about feelings of humiliation.

We don't know a whole lot about this little man, Zacchaeus, but we
do know he was physically small—to get a view of Jesus he had to climb a
tree!

We'll never know what it was about Zacchaeus that attracted Jesus'
attention. Maybe it was simply the fact that Zacchaeus had made the effort
to climb into a tree. We *do* know Jesus noticed this little man and spoke
directly to him: 'Zacchaeus, hurry and come down; for I must stay at your
house today.'[1] Is it too much to suggest that Zacchaeus represents all those
whose smallness stops them from developing? I'm not just referring to those
who are physically small, I'm thinking of all those whose experiences of life

have made them feel small and humiliated; those who have felt so belittled that they have come to hate themselves.

I suspect a large number of people would fit into that category:

- those who have been abused, emotionally or physically
- those whose parents made them feel that their acceptance was proportionate to their achievement
- those who have experienced deep rejection from someone they deeply loved
- those whose sexual orientation has left them feeling rejected
- those who are poor in an affluent society
- those who have been caught doing what is wrong

The list could go on and on...

Are we to say that such people are under a life sentence? Sadly, many seem to be. In order to cope they manufacture behaviour to compensate for their sense of smallness. Some of them 'act big', becoming aggressive and intolerant of others. Some will invent behaviour designed to get attention, which usually results in the opposite of what was intended. Others will be so disabled by all this that they will require specialist counselling to help them. But there will be some for whom an encounter with love will start the process of repair.

It was the encounter that Zacchaeus had with Jesus, the Son of God, that started a turnaround that at one level is difficult to explain. We are not told whether Zacchaeus' recovery was long-term or just a short-term remission, but what we *do* know is that the acceptance Zacchaeus felt from Jesus had a dramatic effect.

How will people encounter Jesus today, given that his physical presence is no longer with us? For some, I suspect a few, a 'direct' spiritual experience will set this process in motion. For others, the love of Jesus will need to be evident in more tangible form. It will need to be revealed for them through Christians.

I hesitate to offer the example of Mother Teresa, as our immediate response to this woman of huge stature (though physically tiny) is our usual, 'I could never be like that.' However, I believe her costly commitment to those around her is something that we Christians are too quick to avoid. Our society abounds with damaged people; people who feel humiliated and rejected; people who feel small. If God is to bring healing to these individuals and to us, he may well require us to supply some unswerving, unconditional love. Too often we are quick to label people as 'problems'. Jesus never did this. Rather, he looked at people in terms of their potential. Maybe we need to start looking at life's 'problem people' through God's eyes, looking at them again and constantly reminding ourselves that we are not perfect either. The difficult thing for us to grasp is that our half-commitment to others is never enough. Those who have become damaged on life's journey are expecting others to reject them. They will even act out behaviours to test our commitment to them. That is why our half-commitment is never enough.

Some years ago a young man arrived on my doorstep at midnight. He explained to me that he had been living with his girlfriend at her parents' home. That evening he had beaten her, and her parents, quite justifiably, had thrown him out. Thus he arrived on my doorstep with nowhere to stay the night and no money. To be truthful, I didn't look at him that night in terms of his potential. As he told me his story I was rapidly trying to invent excuses to get him off my doorstep. Surely it would be lunacy to offer him a bed in my home. In the end, largely because my wife and children were away and I was too tired to invent a 'Grade A' excuse, I allowed him to sleep in our sitting room in a sleeping bag on the sofa.

I awoke next morning expecting the young man to have disappeared with anything and everything of value. But he was there, and we ate breakfast together talking about his life and mine. Our lives had some similarities and one major difference—I had encountered Christ, and he had not. After breakfast he left.

The next time I saw him was at a Christian conference. This same young man flung his arms round me and reminded me of the above incident. He explained that our meeting had started what was for him a life-changing experience. He is now in full-time Christian ministry.

I do not recount that incident because it makes me feel good. I tell it because slightly reluctantly I took a risk for God and he honoured it. To be completely truthful, there have been other times when I have taken risks which have not worked out.

We need to take a few risks for God. We need to risk investing some love in some of life's 'little' people in order that they and we might discover our own stature in God's eyes.

11

GET A LIFE!

When Jesus came to the place, he looked up and said to him, 'Zacchaeus, hurry and come down...'

Luke 19:5

When the tax inspector decides to give half of his possessions away to the poor and to pay back four times over any moneys gained by dubious practice, something's going on! Luke tells us something significant about this funny little man, Zacchaeus. He tells us that out of a confrontation with Jesus there was a changed life.

The issue of change is an interesting one; not least when the Church of which I am a part seems so utterly resistant to it! It must be one of the enigmas of our Christian faith that the religion of Jesus, whose ministry had a very radical edge to it, is more readily associated today with an ill-thought-out conservatism. One wonders how long Jesus would have lasted in many of our churches without being seen as a problem.

Here lies the predicament of the Church. It is difficult for our unchurched friends with their easily aroused cynicism to believe in the life-changing power of the gospel. Unless they see it in the Church, where will they see it? The New Testament is, however, persistent in its evidence that those who met with Jesus found their lives changed. Zacchaeus is just one of those people.

It seems to me that one of the most compelling pieces of evidence for the power of the message about Jesus is that of changed lives. This fact alone is uncomfortable for us because it raises the question as to what extent that transformation is evident within our own lives. It would seem a great pity if the only evidence we could point to of the radically transforming power of the Holy Spirit was in the lives of others.

What is God looking for in our lives? He is looking for a relationship. He wants to know whether we have responded to his love, made available to us in Jesus and evidenced by the cross. But is that it? In John's Gospel Jesus makes a great point: 'Those who abide in me and I in them will bear much fruit.'[1] God is looking for fruit in our lives! He is looking for evidence of growth. Paul gives us an example of the kind of produce that God desires: 'love, joy, peace, patience, kindness, generosity, faithfulness, gentleness and self-control'.[2]

In talking about the positive aspects of being a Christian, I would want to stress that being a follower of Christ does offer us the possibility of real transformation in our lives. To put it another way, I've always felt that those who are entirely happy with the way they are (no one I have yet met!) would have little interest in the Good News about Jesus.

Does that mean that God is seeking perfection? Well, in one way he is. However, it seems to me significant that what God is also looking for is people who will be courageous and tenacious enough to admit their need for personal transformation and open their lives to allow God's Holy Spirit to set about that process. It should be added that when Jesus told his followers, 'Those who abide in me and I in them will bear much fruit', he then said, 'because apart from me you can do nothing'. In a world full of what are known as 'self-help' groups this is a challenging thought. Personal transformation can come with the assurance of divine help.

Of course, it doesn't mean that Christianity has the monopoly on change. I am constantly amazed at the ability of some people to summon up the resources from somewhere to make adjustments to their lives. But if there were the possibility of some power on high wouldn't they be foolish not to avail themselves of it?

Take Zacchaeus for a moment. Here was a man people very probably looked at through the eyes of criticism—even hatred. Those responsible for collecting taxes are rarely popular, but with Zacchaeus there was an extra complication. Not only did he collect taxes, but he did so on the part of the occupying Roman army. In World War II parlance he was what was known as a 'collaborator', hated by his fellow countrymen and prone to overtaxing in order to 'feather his own nest'.

The way we look at others tends to affect the way others behave. Those of us who are parents realize that the way we look at our children can affect the way they turn out. Stephen Covey illustrates this well in his book *The Seven Habits of Highly Effective People*.[3] He writes movingly about how he and his wife regarded one of their children as a failure in need of their protection. When they decided that they would try and look differently at this child and not collude with failure and the need for protection, the child, who had come to rely on their protection, found life difficult at first. In the long term, however, he was transformed into an exceptional achiever with a balanced personality. Covey, in concluding this account, writes: 'We began to realize that if we wanted to change the situation (i.e. our son), we first had to change ourselves.' This is an important perception as so often I find myself thinking that the best way to change a situation is to try to pressurize, even bully, others into change.

The New Testament tells us of Jesus' confrontation with Zacchaeus: 'When Jesus came to the place [that is, the tree Zacchaeus had climbed], he *looked up* and said...' I see this as crucial. For the first time in a very long time someone looked at Zacchaeus through the eyes of love. In that moment something changed in Zacchaeus' life. All the potential, all the mercy, all the sheer goodness were released. Things took place that would never happen whilst Zacchaeus was only looked upon with hatred.

Many people today make comments like, 'I'm too old to change', and it wouldn't surprise me if Zacchaeus hadn't said or thought this himself. The good news is that we're never too old to be changed. We need to lay hold on this truth, that for many that process of change will never begin until they feel the loving gaze of God—which presupposes we've experienced it ourselves.

12

REST ASSURED?

Come to me, all you that are weary and are carrying heavy burdens, and I will give you rest.

Matthew 11:28

I'm always amazed at the amount of luggage we take on holiday with us! That's partly because I'm part of the problem, for, although my intention is to travel light, I regularly end up encumbered by a large and heavy suitcase. It's a great feeling to either have it loaded into the boot of the car or sent down the chute at the airport check-in. Carrying luggage around is a burdensome and tedious business.

If that is true of holiday luggage, what about the luggage we carry through life? Those experiences from the past which weigh us down and limit us in the present. Almost without exception each of us carries his or her own 'luggage' through life. Here is the problem. Just as carrying our holiday luggage limits our movement and progress, so travelling on life's journey with hearts and minds filled with emotional baggage is equally debilitating. It stunts our development and hinders our personal growth.

Many individuals attend sessions with trained counsellors in an attempt to offload some of life's luggage. As far as I can see, counselling can be of great value in this way. Some of us attend 'self-help' groups to try and dump some of those excess bags, and I know of people who have really felt that they were able to unburden themselves in this way. Some of us have the kind of relationships where our friends help us to struggle through life.

Jesus, the Son of God, makes an extraordinary offer. To those who are weighed down with life's luggage he offers to come and give a hand: 'Come to me, all you that are weary and are carrying heavy burdens, and I will give you rest.'[1]

One of the tragedies of life's luggage is that it stops us reaching our true potential as human beings. In fact I think we get more from life when we commit ourselves to reaching that true potential. One of the 'added values' of a Christian faith is that we allow the possibility of God's assistance in helping us to reach our potential as human beings.

How many people can you think of who have great gifts and abilities but whose character gets in the way of their utilizing those gifts and abilities in any meaningful way? So often we see this with our colleagues, our children and other members of our family. God is principally interested in our character. That's why the Bible is full of wisdom regarding character formation. That 'luggage' needs dealing with.

This is not the same as saying 'Come to Jesus and all your problems will be over.' The formation of character is a painful long-term business not a 'quick-fix' solution. When children are ill and attend the doctor's surgery they are usually fine until the doctor does something they don't like. It may be sticking one of those horrid wooden spatulas in their mouth to look down their throat or, even worse, it might be the sudden appearance of a syringe. In other words, our children are mostly happy to commit themselves to the doctor until it looks as though what is about to happen might hurt! At that point they want to call off the appointment even though what the doctor has in mind is in their best interest.

When it comes to character building we can be exactly the same. In theory we commit ourselves to a process, but if it starts to look as though it may be painful we start to retreat or change the subject in order to avoid the pain. The trouble is there is no 'quick-fix' solution, though we all wish there were. Character building takes time and courage. That's why so many shy away from it.

It's true of a good number of us and therefore likely to be true of others that we find it hard to own the fact that we carry luggage around with us, many of us for years. That is part of the genius of Jesus in saying, 'Come to me.' He knew that we would find it difficult to admit our need of help and this is why he places the onus on us. 'If you want help it's up to you to start the process...' is in effect what he is saying.

One of the attractions of Christian faith is that it earths our lives in twin realities. The first, the huge potential of every human being on the planet to know that 'I am fearfully and wonderfully made',[2] is to point us powerfully in the direction of our potential. Every human being has the ability to make a difference. Every human being has the potential to do immeasurable good (or harm!) to his or her fellow creatures.

The second reality that Christianity helps me understand is that though we are uniquely made with individual gifts, strengths and weaknesses, we find it very difficult in our own strength to reach that potential. That's partly because realizing that potential demands discipline, honesty and courage. Jesus says that if we come to him he'll help us carry our luggage. In fact, he took that luggage to a cross and 'threw it down the chute' so that our journey in life might not be hindered, that we might strive unhindered to become the people God wants us to be.

My good friend, Stuart Robinson, tells the story of a gifted violinist who frequently played his Stradivarius violin at concerts. People would listen to the exquisite music he played and extol the virtues of the tone of the violin. One day the same violinist found an old and battered violin in a junk shop. That instrument, in contrast to the Stradivarius, was worth almost nothing. Painstakingly he restored the battered violin until it was ready to be played in a public place. At the end of the concert members of the audience were heard to say 'Doesn't the Stradivarius sound wonderful!' In the hands of the master the potential of the instrument was reached.

In the hands of the Master will our true potential be reached?

Jesus says: 'Come to me, all you that are weary and are carrying heavy burdens, and I will give you rest.'

13

PAYING THE FARE

> Now the word of the Lord came to Jonah son of Amittai,
> saying, 'Go at once to Nineveh, that great city, and cry
> out against it... But Jonah set out to flee to Tarshish
> from the presence of the Lord. He went down to Joppa
> and found a ship going to Tarshish; so he paid his fare
> and went on board...

Jonah 1:1–3

There is a popular viewpoint heard today when our society attempts to tackle the somewhat knotty problem of morality. It goes something like this: 'As long as what you do feels all right and it doesn't harm anyone else, it's fine!' Those exact words may not actually be used, but in essence that's the spirit of the age.

It is puzzling to look at our society today. We are better fed, better housed, and better educated than ever before. But, in spite of all these positive aspects, there remains the difficult question as to why we seem to be in such a mess. You would imagine, given all that society has to offer, that we would be seeing some real quality in the nature of it. Instead, we are aware that we are living in times as morally confused, violent and selfish as at any time in history. Asking the question 'why' brings forth a variety of answers. I was struck by the words of one GP writing in the *Daily Telegraph* after the death in February 1993 of little James Bulger, the toddler murdered in Liverpool by two ten-year-olds:

> *The evident fact is that a high percentage of our children are growing up without any spiritual or cultural framework whatever. In this sense, the murder of James Bulger was not surprising; it was only an extreme example of the brutality to be expected in a moral void.*

There has been recent talk of a return to teaching morality in the classroom.

Many Christians will 'throw their hats in the air' at such news. But what kind of morality? Which criteria will be used to decide what is moral? Who will make these decisions? The plot, as they say, thickens.

Some while ago a panel of people on a radio talk show were asked which characters from history they would most like to meet. I have no recollection of what any of them said, but it set my mind thinking who I would like to meet. Amongst others, I decided I would like to meet Jonah. I have always imagined that he was a real character with a wonderfully human side to his nature. Unlike many of us, Jonah was apparently very receptive to knowing exactly what God wanted him to do. But like many of us he was prone to doing the opposite! When God said to Jonah, 'Go to Nineveh', Jonah managed to find a standby ticket on a boat heading in the opposite direction. Does this ring any bells in your head?

Whatever sin is, Jonah, like many of us, thought he could handle it. He is, therefore, a lively example of that tendency which resides within us all. I don't suppose that he took any counsel in making his 'bad call', but I can imagine a good number of people would have been entirely supportive of his blatant disobedience. After all, it felt good to Jonah and it didn't seem as though it would hurt anyone.

In the third verse there hides a telling phrase in this funny book, best known for the man-eating fish that greeted Jonah after he was thrown overboard by the sailors. The writer of the Book of Jonah records these words: 'So he [Jonah] paid his fare and went on board, to go with them to Tarshish.' I read these words time and time again over the years before it became clear to me *why* the author included them. Suddenly it hit me! The moral of this part of Jonah's story is this: when we decide to go our way and not God's way, we always end up paying the price.

I do not believe it is possible to sin in a vacuum. The fact is that when I do something wrong, I end up paying the price. However, the book's message at this point is even more alarming. For Jonah's wrongdoing did not just cost him a standby, one-way ticket to Tarshish—it almost cost his life and the lives of his travelling companions. It is important that we understand this. The argument that 'it doesn't hurt anyone else' to justify our behaviour suddenly looks a little fragile.

Paul, writing to the Christians at Galatia, makes the point clearly:

Do not be deceived; God is not mocked, for you reap whatever you sow.
If you sow to your own flesh, you will reap corruption from the flesh; but
if you sow to the Spirit, you will reap eternal life from the Spirit.[1]

The problem with programmes to teach morality is that they are never enough. On their own they are unlikely to deliver. The reason for this is that such programmes don't take seriously enough what the Bible says about humanity, which is that human beings are innately self-centred, sinful creatures. To that extent programmes attempting to teach morality can be likened to a surgeon simply sticking plasters on a patient whose injuries are internal and life-threatening—well-intentioned but unlikely to help.

If it is not possible to sin in a vacuum, it is equally impossible to teach morality in a vacuum. Such teaching needs to be accompanied by motivational, cultural and ideological/theological foundations which will provide a firm basis for the practice of such morality.

I suspect that both in our society and within the Church we have effectively played down the consequences of sinful behaviour. Jonah's experience could be mirrored time and time again by many individuals. With Jonah we know that our wrongdoing has not only jeopardized our own well-being, but very often the well-being of others around us.

Part of the Good News about Jesus is that he offers us a way to break both the power and the consequences of our sin. Chapter 3 of the Book of Jonah, written years before the death of Christ, makes the offer of a new start to Jonah perfectly clear: 'The word of the Lord came to Jonah a second time.'[2]

Thankfully, God gives us a second chance. Indeed, he gives us every chance in this life to respond to him and break the power and consequences of our sinfulness. Jonah, like many of us, had to learn the hard way that ignoring God is a destructive option. I sense our godless society needs to learn a similar lesson.

14

FREE OFFER?

**For the wages of sin is death, but the free gift of God is
eternal life in Christ Jesus our Lord.**

Romans 6:23

Our experience of life mostly teaches us to be cautious of free offers. Some
years ago this was exemplified perfectly on a television programme when a
well-known personality attempted to give away £5 notes in a shopping mall.
Almost without exception those who were offered the money declined to
take it. Why? Because they thought there would be a hidden snag. As they
say, 'There is no such thing as a free lunch!' When there is talk of a free
offer, the majority are sceptical.

It is partly because of this fact that a lot of people easily become nervous
of God's free offer made to us in the person of Jesus Christ upon the cross
of Calvary. When those of us who are preachers speak about the *free* offer
that God makes, many people, I suspect, are instantly sceptical. Everything
in them tells them that any free offer has to be taken with a pinch of salt.
They are immediately looking for the small print, trying to discover what
the real story is. The good news is that God's offer comes free of small
print!

The implication of Paul's teaching is twofold. First, as we recalled in the
last chapter, sin has a consequence. Paul describes that consequence as
death. This, of course, does not just refer to physical death—we don't drop
dead the moment we sin! Our sinfulness, however, makes us spiritually
dead; it inhibits our relationship with God.

Nowhere is this made more clear than in the early chapters of the book
of Genesis. The man and woman in the garden are given freedom to do
what they like in that beautiful place. There was only one stipulation: they
were warned not to partake of the fruit from the tree in the middle of
the garden. This warning was backed up by a threat: 'You shall not... touch
it, or you shall die.'[1] We know, of course, that the woman succumbed to

temptation and encouraged the man to eat some of the appealing fruit. Despite the threat, they did not die—not straight away.

The point is that at that stage their fellowship with God was broken. They were, as Paul wrote elsewhere, 'dead through... trespasses and sins'.[2] Indeed, their immediate response to what they had done was to try to hide from God.[3] Goodness knows there are enough people all around us trying to do exactly that!

This death that is the direct result of our wrongdoing helps explain why so many speak of a sense of God's remoteness. Even those of us who are Christians know that if we repeatedly do wrong things we experience a similar distance opening up between ourselves and God. In a world where morality has become both subjective and individualistic—'I felt OK with what I did'—it is little wonder that our society seems increasingly godless.

The second implication of Paul's teaching is much more positive: 'The free gift of God is eternal life in Christ Jesus our Lord.'[4] Paul is saying here that there is a way in which we can avoid the long-term damage that our sinfulness will inflict upon us. How? 'In union with Christ Jesus', the free gift becomes ours. What is that gift? It is the gift of eternal life. What seems threatening to many is the fact that the offer is free. It is limited, but it is free. Limited in the sense that it is only accessible to those who are 'in union with Christ Jesus'. Free in the sense that it cannot be bought or earned. The price has already been paid by Jesus on the cross of Calvary. It is there, Paul tells us, without explaining fully the mystery of how it happens—probably because he could not explain such a mystery—'that Christ died for our sins in accordance with the scriptures'.[5]

You would imagine that such an offer would immediately be of great interest and fascination to a large number of people. Strangely the reverse would seem to be true. So many of those who own a faith in Christ appear to have very little handle on eternity. Many more remain apparently indifferent. Why would this be? For some, ignorance of what God is offering has shaped their indifference. For some, the free nature of God's offer is itself a stumbling block. They would prefer to 'earn' their place in heaven by trying to live a good life without ever knowing how good they might need to become. Others are put off by a fear that eternal life might mean the endless continuation of life as it is in the here and now. Not surprisingly, the idea of such a heaven has an extremely limited appeal!

The promise of eternal life is something that we Christians need reminding of, never mind our unchurched friends. To receive the gift of eternal life is to bring an incredible perspective which seems to be missing in many of our lives. Coping with life's adversity and with physical death in ourselves or in others whom we love is given a new perspective when we fully understand both the nature and the basis of God's free offer.

One of the significant impacts made by the Christians within the early Church, often hounded, tortured and killed by those around them, was the way in which they faced death. Justin the Philosopher, born in AD110, says that he, like Tertullian, was astonished and moved 'when I saw Christians... fearless of death'.[6] Eventually Justin found amongst the early Christian community what he had vainly sought for years in philosophy; that fearlessness in the face of death was inspired by their unshakeable conviction that God's offer of eternal life was for real.

To some extent what we believe about our death will affect the way we go about our lives. If I believe that death is the end, or that the quality of my life after death will be shaped by the quality of my effort before death (reincarnation), these beliefs will influence my approach to my life. If death is the end, then I might as well 'eat, drink and be merry, for tomorrow we die'. But what if I am wrong? Alternatively, having to trust in my own efforts to secure some kind of reasonable afterlife brings an uncertainty about how well I might be doing or not doing!

I sense that our reluctance within our churches to talk about such issues has left us with a devalued gospel. We may fear to talk of such things to those we meet because we fear it will unearth a set of questions we couldn't begin to answer. But does it matter if we can't answer every question we are asked? I believe that God can use an honest 'don't know' rather than a trite or superficial attempt to answer a question we don't really know the answer to. My experience as a preacher tells me that people, like Justin the Philosopher, are looking anywhere and everywhere for something to believe that makes sense of both life and death. Will they, like Justin, find it within the Christian community?

15

GETTING THE MOST OUT OF LIFE

I came that they may have life, and have it abundantly.

John 10:10

Before my own conversion to Christianity I had very little knowledge of either the Christian faith or the Church. What I did have were certain perceptions of both. These were formed, not by Christians I knew, because I really didn't know any that well, neither were they fashioned by any great knowledge of the Church. I had attended confirmation classes, but sporadically. Although I realized that being confirmed was important, 'getting done' was far more of an occasion for my relatives rather than a significant spiritual landmark in my own life. Any recollection of the actual confirmation service was that of a non-event.

What is interesting, and essential to remember when dealing with our unchurched friends, is that my perceptions were negative and held with conviction. You might well guess that those views were neither accurate nor flattering, but they existed nevertheless. I suspect that my experiences as an unchurched youth were not just common to me. There are many people who, on the basis of very little data, have highly developed and largely negative perceptions of the Church and, in consequence, of the Christian faith. How I viewed the Church could be summarized as follows:

- a woman's world, not for men
- boring, irrelevant and out of touch with people
- inhabited by people who were not like me. I was not, nor ever could be, good enough
- culturally imperialistic. It felt as though you had to like a certain kind of music and language in order to belong
- self-righteous

In consequence I thought the Christian faith was:

• **negative and disapproving**
• **out to curb enjoyment**
• **for weak people**
• **'mumbo-jumbo' earthed neither in truth nor reality**

Some years ago I conducted some limited research into unchurched people's perceptions of the Church. Their response had a high degree of resonance with my own feelings. Looking at the list of negative perceptions above, I can see that my ideas about the Church had deeply influenced my ideas about the Christian faith. I can also see that, sadly, many churches seem to go out of their way to reinforce a negative image of themselves. Part of my struggle as a young Christian was to persist with churches which seemed to confirm my worst suspicions. Even now, looking at those perceptions with reference to the Church, I shudder to reflect on how much of what we do in our churches simply colludes with people's low expectations.

What, of course, have undoubtedly changed are my perceptions of the Christian faith. I now see how very wide of the mark they were. None of these would I now remotely accept.

The reason I write about this is because we need to understand that most unchurched people are not in neutral when it comes to thinking about the Church and Christianity. They are not necessarily hostile—neither was I—but they are suspicious and extremely doubtful as to whether Christianity or the Church has got anything to offer them. It is often at times when those expectations and perceptions are disturbed that people become surprisingly receptive. That can happen at a baptism or a wedding or a funeral. It can happen when we decide to break the mould, commit ourselves to our unchurched friends and allow the Holy Spirit to use us.

A surprisingly common view (but not held by believers, I trust) is that Christianity might diminish one's enjoyment of life, that becoming a Christian would entail giving up so much that the colour of life would rapidly become monochrome. That's an attitude we need to dent!

In part, it will be dented by what our unchurched friends see in our lives. It will also be dented by their being confronted by the promises of Jesus, with a challenge to them to respond to the risk of faith in him. In John

10:10, Jesus offers a promise which has particular relevance to all this: 'I came that they [my followers] may have life and have it abundantly.'

It is certainly true that becoming a follower of Christ will entail some personal sacrifices. There were plenty to be made in my life! But the risk of faith challenges us to trust that in bringing our lives under the lordship of Jesus, we shall discover an enjoyment and fulfilment in life that can be found nowhere else. That doesn't mean that the Christian life is easy. It does mean that 'in Christ' we shall find a new joy and a deep sense of satisfaction.

When the Christian Church was born, on the Jewish festival of Pentecost, St Luke tells us that the Spirit came upon the believers. Miraculously they were empowered to speak in a new way about the amazing things God had done. The church in Jerusalem grew that day. However, some of the crowd, endowed with cynical minds, mocked those Christians, accusing them of being drunk. I imagine that their joy on that extraordinary day was so unrestrained and spontaneous that something in their behaviour reflected the 'merriness' and lack of self-consciousness that is so commonly seen in too much alcohol.[1]

Some years ago a popular T-shirt slogan stated in large capital letters: 'CHOOSE LIFE'. A decision for Christ is a decision for abundant life. If that's a message we can't communicate with our lips and our lives, we shall simply reinforce the perceptions of our unchurched friends.

16

LEARNING TO TRUST GOD

'Have faith in God.'

Mark 11:22

Bruce Larsen in his book *Dare to Live Now* records this incident:

The following letter was found in a baking powder tin wired to the handle of an old pump that offered the only hope of drinking water on a very long and seldom used trail across the Amargosa Desert:

> *'This pump is all right as of June 1932. I put a new sucker washer into it and it ought to last five years. But the washer dries out and the pump has got to be primed. Under the white rock I buried a bottle of water, out of the sun and cork end up. There's enough water in it to prime the pump, but not if you drink some first. Pour about one fourth and let her soak to wet the leather. Then pour in the rest medium fast and pump like crazy. You'll get water. The well has never run dry. Have faith. When you get watered up, fill the bottle and put it back as you found it for the next feller.*
>
> *(signed) Desert Pete*
>
> *P.S. Don't go drinking up the water first. Prime the pump with it and you'll get all you can hold.'*[1]

What does having faith mean? Often people will claim to 'have faith'. Mostly it is faith in a person: 'I've got great faith in my doctor.' Sometimes it is used with reference to people of a religious disposition: 'I wish I had their faith.' But what is faith? Is it, as one young boy was heard to define, believing the unbelievable? It's a word used often by Christians, but it is surprising how little clarity there is on what we actually mean by it!

Everyday living means that we employ trust in others. Relationships where there is little or no trust quickly founder. When we commit ourselves to experts we have to trust their expertise. If the 'little man' who fixes our car tells me I need a new thermostat I trust him. I have never seen an atom or a molecule, but I accept they exist because eminent scientists tell me they do.

Desert Pete's letter is an excellent example of what faith is. The action ensuing when a tired and thirsty traveller discovered that note would be indicative of their faith. Within our own culture we have made faith seem like the acceptance of a set of intellectual propositions. To think like that is not wrong, but it is not the whole picture. Faith is not just the outcome of academic discussion, neither is leaving our brains in the church porch a good way to go about our Christianity either. The letter from Desert Pete illustrates perfectly what faith is about.

Faith always has an object. When St Mark recorded Jesus as saying 'Have faith in God',[2] the grammar of the Greek emphasizes God as the object of our faith. Faith always has an object. In the letter above Desert Pete is faith's object. In terms of our Christian faith the object of our faith is God as revealed to us in Jesus. In essence faith describes a relationship of trust rather than an acceptance of propositions. It is faith in a person.

In today's world I think this is difficult. There is a widespread recognition that within society there is a growing percentage of people who have been damaged. The upsurge in broken homes has left many spouses and their offspring feeling rejected and hurt. For them the issue of ever placing trust in others again is a matter of great inner struggle. The demand of faith is therefore a scary business. Before they will entrust themselves to anybody ever again they will need to feel that there are firm grounds for trust. Indeed before they trust, they may need to know a measure of healing in their lives.

It is for this reason that there is great emphasis in the Bible upon God being both faithful and trustworthy. As the psalmist reminds us, 'The Lord exists forever; your word is firmly fixed in heaven. Your faithfulness endures to all generations.'[3] God knows that trusting others is difficult and so his word offers us ample evidence that he is trustworthy. In the end, like the traveller finding Desert Pete's note, you have to make up your own mind.

In one way, to say that faith must have an object is a pretty obvious comment. However, it's important for us to remember this because there is a subtle trap into which we can easily fall. St Mark encourages us to have faith in God. There is a tendency that we need to be aware of: we are always in danger of having faith in faith.

Our innate sense as human beings is that we do not have enough faith. When in life we are faced with a problem we 'get out' what faith we have and examine it. We recognize that it is small and we immediately feel disabled. Ronald Dunn, preaching on Mark 11:22, makes the same point: 'It is very significant that Jesus' emphasis is not on faith, but on its object.'[4] That great Baptist preacher, Spurgeon, said: 'Don't make a Christ of your faith.' Almost all those who sought Jesus' help came with a feeble and imperfect faith.

A definition of faith is perfectly illustrated in Desert Pete's letter, as it is in the lives of the saints throughout the years. Faith is taking God at his word and acting as though we do. To access the promise of unlimited water in the illustration, travellers would have to believe what Desert Pete had written. But that would not be enough. There is not only something to believe, there is something to do: ACT ON THE PROMISE, that is, carry out the instructions in the written note. I think this is what James was trying to express when he wrote, 'Be doers of the word, and not merely hearers who deceive themselves.'[5]

Think for a moment how different our churches would be if Christians held this dynamic view of faith! Imagine how exciting our lives would be if we trusted God in this way. It is reassuring for us to recall that Jesus indicated that the amount of our faith need not be huge for us to achieve great things.

The apostles said to the Lord, 'Increase our faith!' The Lord replied, 'If you had faith the size of a mustard seed, you could say to this mulberry tree, "Be uprooted and planted in the sea," and it would obey you.'[6]

17

LIVING WITH LIFE'S UNANSWERED QUESTIONS

How long, O Lord? Will you forget me forever? How long will you hide your face from me?

Psalm 13:1–2

On a noticeboard outside a church was written, 'JESUS IS THE ANSWER.' In felt-tip pen beneath, someone had added the words, 'What's the question?' There is a sort of game being played out here. On the one hand, the Church is looked to for answers to some of life's big questions; on the other hand, it seems it is often answering questions that no one is asking. At the same time, the answers given are not always those that people want to hear!

Those of us who have ever had any experience of working with young people, either as parents or professionally, know only too well that sometimes when the young ask a question they do not want to hear the answer that is given. So often the questions begin with, 'Is it OK if I...?' The snag is that it is often not OK!

Whatever our experience of life, whether we are of a religious disposition or not, life itself throws up a great number of questions. Many of these are answered in the classrooms and lecture theatres of our educational establishments, but others are not. Part of the reason for this is that there are some questions to which an answer just cannot be given. The situation is further exacerbated by the fact that so many of the unanswerable questions in life are those that have the greatest significance for us.

At a personal level, when things go wrong in our lives we find ourselves asking 'Why?' When I was in my early twenties, I was involved in a road accident in which an attractive young woman received appalling facial injuries. The accident happened on a quiet section of a main road when someone turned out of a side road without stopping and the vehicle I was driving hit theirs almost head-on. I remember thinking that, given the quietness of the road, the odds of two cars colliding with each other like that were somewhat unlikely. I was left asking, 'Why?' Why did it have to happen? Why was I involved? And I admit I also asked, 'What did I do to deserve this?' These are the sort of very human questions we ask when faced with life's adversities. The way we handle such questions will leave us either embittered or able to work such experiences into the warp and weft of our existence and survive them.

Leaving behind the personal aspect of adversity, to think about the 'bigger picture', is to see our questions proliferate. Why do such terrible things happen in our world? When such instances hit the headlines we are, it seems, destined to be overwhelmed by 'why?' The customary answers rarely seem satisfactory and are often regarded as only trite and inadequate.

In the Old Testament book of Job we are introduced to a man in the depths of personal suffering. After losing his personal wealth and his family through natural disasters (called 'acts of God' by insurance companies!), Job was understandably tormented by a whole raft of 'why?' questions.

- 'Why did I not die at birth?'[1]
- 'Why was I not buried like a stillborn child?'[2]
- 'Why is light given to one in misery, and life to the bitter in soul, who long for death, but it does not come?'[3]

Initially, Job's friends adopted the wise approach and for seven days nothing was said.[4] In the face of unanswerable questions, silence is often a powerful thing. Indeed, it was when Job's so-called 'comforters' opened their mouths that their role as comforters was seriously undermined!

W.H. Auden wrote, 'To ask the hard question is simple.'[5] In other words, the asking of a question is the easy part. Finding an appropriate answer is more difficult. As we go through life, more and more questions arise. The frustration is that not as many answers are forthcoming.

One of the privileges of a life lived by faith is the potential to learn to live with life's unanswered questions. Our willingness to entrust ourselves to God is, in part, a recognition that we cannot ourselves understand all things. To trust in the ultimate goodness of God is to believe that although much of what we see appears unjust, out of control and without purpose, there will be a time when all that is unjust will be rectified, all that is unclear will become clearer, and the purposes of God will never be derailed.

Though what we experience and feel may often appear to contradict it, we continue to trust that God is all those things that the Bible tells us he is.

Chapter 13 of 1 Corinthians is significantly one of the best-known chapters in the whole Bible because of its meditation on the nature and permanence of love. It is easy to miss the timeless wisdom encapsulated in the second half of the chapter: 'When I was a child, I spoke like a child, I thought like a child, I reasoned like a child; when I became an adult, I put an end to childish ways. *For now we see in a mirror, dimly, but then we will see face to face. Now I know only in part; then I will know fully, even as I have been fully known*' (italics mine).[6]

There are some things that we cannot know. Sometimes it is because of a lack of available knowledge. It may well be that further research will, at some stage in the future, reveal that knowledge to us. The hardest questions to live with are those that people cannot align with any sense of purpose or meaning. They are the 'why?' questions.

The reason why a faith in God is important is that it always brings us back to the issue of ultimate purpose. It offers us a way of making a connection between the 'why?' questions and a purpose that, although not always visible, is in the control and hands of a God who is ultimately loving. As Paul indicates in 1 Corinthians 13, we all have the feeling that, at best, we are looking through a mirror and our knowledge is partial. Faith asks us to hold on to God at times when we cannot make sense of what is going on around us, with the certainty that one day we shall 'know fully'.

Ken Blanchard recalls a story he heard which illustrates well the difference between those who have some sense of purpose and those who do not. 'I recently read a beautiful story that relates to the importance of purpose. Two workers were hammering on a piece of granite with a sledgehammer. When asked what he was doing, the first worker said, "I'm trying to crack this granite." When asked the same question, the second worker said, "I'm part of a team building a cathedral."'[7]

As Christians we are always 'cathedral builders' and not 'granite crackers'. We know that ultimately God's purpose will be worked out. The writer of the book of Proverbs assures us that, 'The human mind may devise many plans, but it is the purpose of the Lord that will be established.'[8]

Donald Sutherland, in his biography of Gertrude Stein, tells us, 'just before she died she asked, "What is the answer?" No answer came. She laughed and said, "In that case what is the question?" Then she died.'[9] I suspect that peace on these matters will come to us only when we accept that there is little doubt that all of us will both live and die with many of our questions unanswered.

> *How long, O Lord? Will you forget me forever?*
> *How long will you hide your face from me?*
> *How long must I bear pain in my soul,*
> *and have sorrow in my heart all day long?*
> *How long shall my enemy be exalted over me?*
> *Consider and answer me, O Lord my God!*
> *Give light to my eyes, or I will sleep the sleep of death,*
> *and my enemy will say, 'I have prevailed';*
> *my foes will rejoice because I am shaken.*
> *But I trusted in your steadfast love;*
> *my heart shall rejoice in your salvation.*
> *I will sing to the Lord,*
> *because he has dealt bountifully with me.*[10]

18

WHEN BAD THINGS HAPPEN
TO GOOD PEOPLE

**My grace is sufficent for you, for power is made perfect
in weakness.**

2 Corinthians 12:9

When Rabbi Harold Kushner wrote his book *When Bad Things Happen to
Good People* it became a bestseller. The reason for this, I think, is obvious.
The statement embraced in the title raises an issue of interest to many people—the question as to the 'why?' of human suffering. This comes into
sharp focus when people whom we would describe as 'good' are the recipients of what we construe as unjust and undeserved suffering. We see the
world in which we live littered with examples of this.

John Stott describes the problem that this kind of adversity gives to
those of us seeking to promote the Christian faith. He writes: 'The fact of
suffering undoubtedly constitutes the single greatest challenge to the
Christian faith, and has been in every generation.'[1] Deep down within us
we Christians know that to be the case. At times when tragedies make the
headlines, it almost feels embarrassing to believe in a God of love. We rightly recoil from saying too much lest it sounds cheap; we struggle to find the
right words to say in case we get it wrong.

St Paul certainly knew what it was to have adversity in his life. To a
church which doubted his claim to be a serious apostle, Paul listed his credentials. Significantly his credentials had more to do with his suffering than
his studies. In 2 Corinthians 11 he parades those qualities for apostleship:

*I have worked much harder, been in prison more frequently, been flogged
more severely, and been exposed to death again and again. Five times I
received from the Jews the forty lashes minus one. Three times I was
beaten with rods, once I was stoned, three times I was shipwrecked, I
spent a night and a day in the open sea...*[2]

I wish there were a simple answer to this kind of suffering, but my experiences of life tell me there isn't one. In part this is what the mystery of suffering is. But there is an aspect to the mystery of suffering which is even more profound. It is to do with the fact that paradoxically it is often in suffering that God reveals himself to men and women. Again, that was Paul's experience: 'a thorn was given me in the flesh, a messenger of Satan to torment me... Three times I appealed to the Lord about this, that it would leave me, but he said to me, "My grace is sufficient for you, for power is made perfect in weakness." '[3]

It is significant that God spoke profoundly to Paul in the midst of his suffering. It may even be questionable whether Paul would have heard God in any other context—we shall never know. What is clear is that in the midst of Paul's suffering, God was there.

One of the most powerful things a Christian can say, at the right time, in the face of human suffering is that the Lord we worship is not remote or dispassionate from our adversity. When we speak about the 'touch of Christ' or the 'hand of God', we must remember that those hands bear the scars of Calvary's cross. A most moving illustration of what I am talking about is recalled by John Stott:

I could never myself believe in God, if it were not for the cross. The only God I believe in is the One Nietzsche ridiculed as 'God on the Cross'. In the real world of pain, how could one worship a God who was immune to it? I have entered many Buddhist temples in different Asian countries and stood respectfully before the statue of the Buddha, his legs crossed, arms folded, eyes closed, the ghost of a smile playing round his mouth, a remote look on his face, detached from the agonies of the world. But each time after a while I have had to turn away. And in imagination I have turned instead to that lonely, twisted, tortured figure on the cross, nails through hands and feet, back lacerated, limbs wrenched, brow bleeding, God-forsaken darkness. That is the God for me! He laid aside his immunity to pain. He entered our world of flesh and blood, tears and death. He suffered for us. Our suffering become more manageable in the light of his. There is still a question mark against human suffering, but over it we boldly stamp another mark, the cross which symbolizes divine suffering.[4]

I was struck by a story I heard recounted about Woodbine Willy, the famous army chaplain from World War I. It is said that he was doing his rounds of the trenches one day after fierce fighting when he came across a young soldier who was badly injured and close to death. Woodbine Willy noticed his lips moving in a feeble attempt to speak and, putting his ear to the young man's mouth, heard him whisper, 'How can your God allow this to happen?' Wisely, Woodbine Willy said nothing, but he unclipped from his belt his crucifix and held before the dying man the body of Christ depicted on the cross. The young soldier stared at the cross. With death imminent he took an intake of breath and said three words: 'Now I understand.' With that he breathed his last and died.

Every time I tell that story I find myself deeply moved. It communicates in a way that I can't the wonder that in our suffering Jesus is there with us. Christ on a cross communicates far more than we shall ever know or understand.

19

GETTING GOD'S HELP

I lift up my eyes to the hills—from where will my help come? My help comes from the Lord, who made heaven and earth.

Psalm 121:1–2

Most people, at some point in their lives, either pray or think about praying. Often the decision to pray is made at times of crisis when we are feeling desperate or hopeless or both. You may have heard the story about a man who was out walking on a coastal path on the edge of cliffs which fell steeply away to the sea. Suddenly he lost his footing and slipped over the cliff edge. Fortunately as he fell he managed to grab hold of a young sapling growing out of the cliff face. As he dangled several hundred feet above a rocky shoreline the sapling slowly began to come away from the face of the cliff. In desperation the man looked heavenward and shouted, 'Is there anyone up there?' To his utter amazement there came a loud and booming voice which said, 'Trust me my son. Let go of the tree and all will be well.' The man reflected briefly and then shouted again, 'Is there anyone else up there?'

The story illustrates well at least two facets of many people's attempts to pray. First, it reminds us that many of our prayers are born from desperation. Second, it raises the fundamental question, 'What is God like?' This is a big issue. Pastoral ministry has made it clear to me that a large number of people are angry with God. They feel that he has let them down in life. At the same time they would like to think that if God does exist, they would want him to be on their side. They would like to believe that prayer works.

Jesus made it clear that our perception of what God is like is important when it comes to this matter of prayer. In a section of teaching on prayer, Jesus concluded, 'Is there anyone among you who, if your child asks for a fish, will give a snake instead of a fish? Or if the child asks for an egg, will give a scorpion? If you then, who are evil, know how to give good gifts to

73

your children, how much more will the heavenly Father give the Holy Spirit to those who ask him!'[1]

Jesus is saying several things here. First, he is telling us that the right context for prayer is relationship. In this context it is a relationship with God. Second, he is saying that this relationship can be compared to a parental relationship. Just as our earthly parents (hopefully) make choices for us that are in our best interests, so our heavenly Father will do the same. Implicitly, therefore, prayer is entrusting ourselves not principally to our list of wants and needs, it is trusting in the ultimate goodness and wisdom of God.

If the context of prayer is a relationship, it figures that it is unlikely that we shall learn to be effective in prayer if our approach to prayer is '999' oriented—emergencies only! Now, I am aware that in his goodness God does respond to 'ambulance' prayers on occasions, but a prayerful approach to life will be better cultivated in an ongoing relationship with God.

At the same time, if that relationship can be described best in parental terms we need to trust that God will always have our best interests at heart. My children constantly bombard me with requests: 'Dad, I need a new bike', 'Dad, can I go on the school trip?' Would it be wise for me to agree to their every request? Of course not. I have to be wise enough to know what kind of response to make to each request. Simply to acquiesce to every request would be to create a 'spoilt brat' culture in our home—over-dependent, over-demanding children. Prayer is not just going to God with a shopping list of demands, only to feel let down when he doesn't immediately respond. A God who did respond like that could make no claim to love us. Part of trusting God is the willingness to believe that he has our well-being as a priority.

It is at this very point that many of us will get stuck. The dominant biblical picture of God as Father can be a stumbling block for those whose earthly fathers were neither loving nor caring. There is an inevitable transference here. If our own experience of being fathered was negative and damaging, it will be harder for us to entrust ourselves to our Father in heaven. In a world where a growing number of people never knew who their real father was and where a lot of fathers are perceived as 'absent' because of their busyness, or worse, where there is abuse, verbal or physical, this is something that we need to bear in mind. All of us find it difficult to learn to trust in God, but for some the task will be further complicated by the legacy of life's experiences.

Some of us are frightened of such things as heights or spiders. We can deal with this in two ways. We can remove ourselves, as far as possible, from situations which would bring us into contact with the object of our fear. This is the route often chosen. Just recently we found one of our daughters sleeping in the guest bedroom because she had seen a large spider in her room the previous evening! Alternatively, we can endeavour to come to terms with our anxiety, and for this we may need some counselling, or someone to be close to us as we try to confront our fear. One thing is clear: while our behaviour is driven by our fears we shall always experience life as less than fulfilling.

Keeping our distance from God because of our fear will always mean that we shall live our lives without the potential that he can bring us. If you were to ask me whether I felt that prayer was a benefit derived from my relationship with God, I would happily affirm it to be so. That does not mean that all my prayers are answered, at least not in a way that is either visible or clear to me. Prayer is a way of expressing faith which is always positive.

Harry Blamires expresses the mystery clearly:

> So when prayer seems difficult and we wonder whether we are being listened to or whether we are talking to ourselves, we need to ask the question, 'What do I expect?' Do I expect, having prayed for my mother's recovery, to hear a divine voice saying, 'Yes, certainly, I'll attend to it straightaway'? Do I expect to see her running downstairs and calling for her golf clubs? And do I expect, having prayed that my cantankerous old neighbour will cease to be so hostile, to find her knocking at the door forthwith, a sweet smile on her face and a bunch of flowers in her hand?
>
> It is when we press the question, 'How could it be otherwise?' that we recognize how exactly right is God's treatment of us.[2]

Read Psalm 121:

> I lift up my eyes to the hills—from where will my help come?
> My help comes from the Lord, who made heaven and earth.
> He will not let your foot be moved; he who keeps you will not slumber.
> He who keeps Israel will neither slumber nor sleep.
> The Lord is your keeper; the Lord is your shade at your right hand.
> The sun shall not strike you by day, nor the moon by night.

The Lord will keep you from all evil; he will keep your life.
The Lord will keep your going out and your coming in from this time on and forevermore.[3]

20

COOPERATING AND COMPETING

**Now you are the body of Christ and individually
members of it.**

1 Corinthians 12:27

There is a very fundamental question related to Christianity that I have
found myself asking. Does my Christian faith make me a more cooperative
than competitive human being? Today's world is undeniably very competitive. In the economic climate of the past few years the value of competition
in economic life has been trumpeted as being beneficial to the producer and
consumer alike. This is not unimportant and would appear to have some
advantages. The fact that manufacturers and service providers know that if
they fall down on price, delivery and customer service, there are others in
the market place who will only too happily take their business has kept such
organizations on their toes.

If we think this competitive emphasis is limited to just the commercial
area of life, however, we are sadly deluded. We can be competitive within
our relationships. 'Keeping up with the Joneses' is demanding stuff. In almost
any context where there are two or more people, or two or more groups of
people, there is always the possibility of competitiveness. It can happen
between married couples and it can occur between massive corporations.
Our overexposure to the model of competition has meant that we have
largely forgotten that there are other models which bear close scrutiny.

The problem with the competition model is that it creates a win/lose
outcome. The assumption that underlies this is that if I win, you lose. My
business might prosper whilst yours declines. When competitiveness gets
completely out of hand, there is always the possibility that we shall be faced
with a lose/lose situation, that is, one which ends up with two losers. Much
of this, of course, is the result of market forces over which we have very little control. When we become highly competitive the atmosphere in which
we try to work becomes extremely stressful. My feeling is that the level of

competition in society has reached a pitch whereby it is causing people real stress. In turn that stress makes us more competitive, and so we are left with a destructive cycle of events and thereby demoralized employees.

In such a climate people find it almost impossible either to cooperate or communicate. If we are to become more cooperative, we will have to learn not to constantly compete with each other. We will need to be motivated to explore different ways of working. Is it too much to suggest that when God created human beings it was his intention that they would be co-operative in their efforts? The writer of Genesis 2 tells us that, 'God took the man and put him in the garden of Eden to till it and keep it.'[1] Almost immediately the narrative tells us that God said, 'It is not good that the man should be alone; I will make him a helper as his partner.'[2]

It was following the Fall that the task of work became sweated labour.[3] In Genesis 4 the story of Cain and Abel makes it clear that discontent and envy can provide a very powerful motivation for competitive behaviour. It also graphically illustrates that such behaviour when taken to extreme lengths can lead to violence and death.[4] All this raises the important questions as to whether we were created to be cooperative and whether it is something related to our fallenness that makes us competitive. Would a redeemed community be a place where cooperation was restored? When we refer to someone as 'naturally competitive', what are we saying, not least in a society that uses such a term as an accolade?

Perhaps we have become so obsessed by the so-called 'advantages' of competition that we find it difficult to even consider other ways of working together. Indeed, we sometimes seem very confused about this whole matter. Managers who encourage their staff to be competitive by setting them individual targets will find it virtually impossible to get those staff members to work together. Churches which are effectively competing within a locality (though they would never own up to it) find it very difficult to work together. If we want to see people working together, which is generally much more rewarding than working competitively, it is no good expecting that to happen within a competitive environment.

Let's be honest. Christians can be as competitive as anyone else. We often compete for attention; we can compete to appear more pious; we can compete for position and status, but we would be hard-pressed to make our Christian beliefs the basis for our competitiveness. Such behaviour usually stems from our insecurity. It is certainly arguable that Christianity is, to a certain extent, the antidote to competitive behaviour. Jesus' emphasis on service,[5] the last being first,[6] put together with Paul's teaching that we should allow the Spirit to develop the 'fruit' of gentleness within us,[7] are serious challenges to the competitive mindset of our times.

Paul's metaphor for the local Christian community as the body of Christ is principally one which speaks about cooperation.[8] In a human body with different parts, the effective working of that body depends on those constituent parts working in harmony with each other. When they don't, there is dysfunction. Those of us who have ever injured a toe or a finger will know that, small as those parts of the body are, they can seriously hinder the working of the whole body. In Paul's thinking, the local church can become a model of cooperative behaviour in a competitive world. It is a scenario in which every person has a part to play. Christianity is no spectator sport!

To each is given the manifestation of the Spirit for the common good.[9]

For just as the body is one and has many members, and all the members of the body, though many, are one body, so it is with Christ. For in the one Spirit we were all baptized into one body.[10]

This collaboration can even transcend those human barriers which normally divide. Within the new community of God's people, ethnic and gender divisions are broken down.[11] Divisions based upon temperament and wealth are abolished.

Some years ago I visited a large church in California. Accompanying me were two businessmen, neither of whom was a Christian. Literally within minutes of the start of the worship, these men were reduced to tears. When I asked them why this was, their answer both shocked and challenged me. They explained that they were deeply moved by the visible unity of what they had seen. Never before had they witnessed rich and poor, black and white, sophisticated and simple, coming together and so evidently enjoying their togetherness. This had had a profound effect on them. Surely that is just one way in which we should be taking the world by surprise.

The more we understand St Paul's metaphor of the body, the more we shall be able to offer the possibility of cooperation in a competitive world. The irony is that the most innovative and creative material I have read on this subject has come from the world of commerce. It seems as the though the limits of competitiveness are beginning to emerge from the pens and word processors of those who previously promoted such a culture. One of those writers is Stephen Covey, who says,

> As with many—many problems between people in business, family, and other relationships—the problem in this company was a flawed paradigm. The president was trying to get the fruits of co-operation from a paradigm of competition. And when it didn't work he wanted a technique, a programme, a quick fix antidote to make his people co-operate.
>
> But you can't change the fruit without changing the root. Working on the attitudes and behaviours would have been hacking at the leaves. So we focused instead on producing personal and organizational excellence in an entirely different way by developing information and reward systems which reinforced the value of co-operation. [12]

Ken Blanchard quotes a poster he saw on a school bulletin board. It read, 'NONE OF US IS AS SMART AS ALL OF US.' [13] The importance of co-operative teamwork in the attainment of goals is important; its contribution to the climate in which people work is crucial. Today's management gurus show an appreciation of this. St Paul, I suggest, got there before them all.

21

FINDING MY GOD-GIVEN POTENTIAL—
THE SECRET OF SUCCESS

The God of heaven is the one who will give us success...

Nehemiah 2:20

Haddon Robinson, the great American preacher, once wrote this: 'Preachers, of course, have to be more than "fellow-strugglers". No one is helped by "You're a loser; I'm a loser; let's keep losing together".'[1] As a preacher those words are a particular challenge to me. They make me think again about the perception that people have of the Church as a place for losers. Those of us who are Christians would probably have to admit that, although we would dispute the label 'losers', we do find it difficult to know how to talk about success within the Christian community.

I have always had the feeling that to speak of a 'successful' element or to ask God for success in our strategies is viewed as distasteful. It may well be that Nehemiah was ignorant of such etiquette, but two things seem clear. First, he wasn't scared to ask God for success in his efforts; second, given the huge task he had set himself—to rebuild the walls of Jerusalem—he was immensely successful, completing the task in record time.

In a world such as ours, dominated by consumerism, people are looking to be successful. They incline to measure their success in terms of their money and possessions. They want successful careers, successful marriages, successful children and successful lifestyles. Because the Church, in this quest for success, seems a hindrance rather than a help it is readily dismissible. Let me make it clear what I am *not* about to argue. I am *not* saying that if only our churches could become success-oriented we would create a better 'sales pitch' in the market place. I am asking whether there is a way of thinking about success which is in line with what God wants in our lives. It appears that the success many chase eludes them, and for the few who consider themselves 'successful' in this world's terms, there appears to be little sense of personal fulfilment.

I want to suggest that success has more to do with fulfilling our potential as human beings than simply measuring our efforts against a set of imposed goals or against the performance of those around us. I think that may be longhand for saying that success is about bringing our lives in line with God's will. I believe we have a better chance of achieving fulfilment in our lives when we do what we were designed to do rather than simply what we think we ought to do.

Concluding the Sermon on the Mount, Jesus said, 'Not everyone who says to me, "Lord, Lord," will enter the kingdom of heaven, but only the one who does the will of my Father in heaven.'[2]

I have always thought that these words are a rebuke by Jesus. But what if he was trying to encourage rather than chastise? Maybe he was, in effect, saying that if the focus of our faith was based in sounding religious or in our status, imagined or real, we would never know the real fulfilment of doing God's will.

I had always envisaged that the Church would be a community within which we would work out together what God's will meant in our lives, both corporately and individually; that it would be a place where we would work out what all Christians need to know. What would my life look like if I made a priority of seeking God's will?

- **What kind of qualities should I work at?**
- **What kind of morality should I model?**
- **What kind of things should I do?**
- **What kind of things should I not do?**
- **What are my gifts?**

Whatever success is, I think it likely that it will come in response to this kind of question, rather than trying to drive myself to greater feats of energy, manipulation, deception, assertiveness and intimidation. Driven people may be successful in the world's eyes, but they are rarely happy. Surely our definition of success must include a degree of happiness and well-being! Stephen Covey makes the same point in a different way:

As my study took me back through 200 years of writing about success, I noticed a startling pattern emerging in the content of the literature. Because of our own pain, and because of similar pain I had seen in the lives and relationships of many people I had worked with through the years, I began to feel more and more that much of the success literature of the past 50 years was superficial. It was filled with social image consciousness, techniques and quick fixes—with social band-aids and aspirin that addressed acute problems and sometimes even appeared to solve them temporarily, but left the underlying chronic problems untouched to fester and resurface time and again.

In stark contrast, almost all the literature in the first 150 years or so focused on what could be called the Character Ethic as the foundation of success—things like integrity, humility, fidelity, temperance, courage, justice, patience, industry, simplicity, modesty, and the Golden Rule. Benjamin Franklin's autobiography is representative of that literature. It is, basically, the story of one man's effort to integrate certain principles and habits deep within his nature.

The Character Ethic taught that there are basic principles of effective living, and that people can only experience true success and enduring happiness as they learn and integrate these principles into their basic character. [3]

The history of Christianity makes mixed reading and there have been some low points. At the same time there has been much good, as shown by the lives of men and women who under the inspiration, motivation and guidance of God's Spirit did amazing things. There have been the men and women, gifted in the creative arts, who inspired by that same Spirit painted, sculpted, composed and wrote, leaving us a priceless legacy of art and culture. Paradoxically Christianity is attributed with creating the intellectual climate out of which grew the scientific quest now so widely and wrongly seen as an enemy of faith. Often this has been the work of men and women who attributed their motivation and inspiration to God.

No one could claim that the route to success through character formation rather than quick-fix techniques is easy. The interface of my wilfulness and God's will is highly uncomfortable; the pursuit of my potential through the nurture and practice of my God-given gifts requires tenacity and persistence. But wouldn't you rather pursue a route to success that, though demanding, led to fulfilment and peace, rather than a quick-fix route that ultimately offered no more than a different kind of emptiness to the one you started out with?

A short while ago I heard someone talking on the radio about how gold becomes the beautiful metal it undoubtedly is. He reminded me that it is mostly the result of a long and frequently disillusioning search; it often involves a bruising and painful encounter with the elements. Finally, if you manage to find some gold ore you have to heat it to a very high temperature to refine it. But presumably it is worth it![4]

22

TAKING MY PART IN THE NEW COMMUNITY

As God's chosen ones, holy and beloved, clothe yourselves with compassion, kindness, humility, meekness, and patience.

Colossians 3:12

I once read an interview with Ian Hislop, editor of the satirical magazine, *Private Eye*. In it he told readers that he was a Christian. He then recalled an incident in a radio interview when the interviewer had pointedly asked him if he was a believer and for reasons known best to himself he denied he was. At that moment of denial he heard a cock crow somewhere inside his head. He later reflected what had made him deny his faith and concluded that he felt that to admit he was a Christian was 'not cool'.

This is a problem we have within the Christian community. In the world's eyes we're 'not cool'. Indeed, I suspect that in the world's eyes we are just a bunch of losers. And that's OK, if a little inhibiting of our mission! Dr Sangster, the Methodist preacher, made a similar point when he apparently told his congregation, 'Do you realize a lot of people are not in church this morning because you are?'

Let's get one thing straight. It is important, within the new community of God's people (the Church), that we are prepared to look realistically and critically at ourselves. That is not because the Church is unimportant; it is because the Church is *very* important. It is a key component in God's strategy to extend his kingdom here on earth. The Church is there to reach people with the good news about God; it is there to assist us to grow towards the likeness of Christ; it is there to worship the living God, not just by handing over an hour of our lives on a Sunday, but by laying down the whole of our lives as an offering to God.

You don't have to have a PhD in theology to recognize the importance and dignity the Bible attributes to the Church. Think about the metaphors used to describe it: 'The Bride of Christ', 'The Body of Christ', 'the people

85

of God', 'the saints at…'. You can be cynical about the Church, and many of us view it as a mixed blessing, but *never* think the Church is unimportant.

That said, it doesn't seem to be very important in the priorities of many of us Christians, never mind the unchurched. As a parish clergyman, on my visits to people in their homes I was so frequently told, 'You don't have to go to church to be a Christian.' At one level I agree with that. It would be nonsense to suggest that going to church made a person a Christian. As Billy Graham has said, 'Going to church doesn't make you a Christian, any more than going to a garage makes you a car.'

Neither is evangelism about 'getting people to come to church'. It's about helping people to establish a relationship with God through Jesus Christ his Son. However, saying that the goal of evangelism is not to get people into church is NOT saying that becoming a member of the new community is unimportant. We need to understand why the Church is necessary for spiritual growth and development. The reason for this is that many people have to get over the 'not cool' feeling in relation to the Church, before they will commit themselves to Christ.

Many ministers and pastors tell me that they rarely meet hostility to Christ, but they frequently encounter hostility towards the Church. People have often said to me, with a worried expression on their faces, 'If I become a Christian, does that mean I *have* to come to church?' Consequently, I want to give some reasons we might give as to why the Church is important. This is not an exhaustive list of qualities of the kind of environment a church should provide, but one which has particular relevance to the development of 'spiritual babes'.

Teaching

The psalmist wrote 'Your word is a lamp to my feet and a light to my path.'[1] Paul wrote to Timothy, a young church leader, 'All scripture is inspired by God and is useful for teaching, for reproof, for correction, and for training in righteousness, so that everyone who belongs to God may be proficient, equipped for every good work.'[2]

It may well be true that Christianity is caught not taught, but if you stop to think about it, Christian discipleship is taught and rarely caught. A lot of the values that God wants his new community to model are not natural to most human beings. We shall need to be trained for discipleship and an important part of that training will mean that we need to expose ourselves to teaching in order that the Holy Spirit may enable us to learn. This doesn't just mean sermons, it might involve small-group learning, but without teaching most spiritual babes stay babes for ever.

Accountability

Mixing with other Christians and forming close relationships offers us the possibility of mutual accountability (the word 'fellowship' carries this meaning). House groups are an important part of this process. They are places where people can love us enough to tell us the truth about ourselves. You don't have to like the experience of someone who cares about you telling the truth, but your development will be very stunted without it. Paul told the Galatians to 'Bear one another's burdens, and in this way you will fulfil the law of Christ.'[3]

Encouragement

Because the Christian life is often tough, many of us are tempted to give it up or create personal defence systems to defuse the radical impact of the gospel on our lives. My experience, both personally and in discipling others, is that a ministry of encouragement is important to the sustained growth of the new community. The writer of the epistle to the Hebrews in the face of a congregation which was in danger of shrinking back[4] wrote these words of advice: 'But encourage one another',[5] or again, 'Let us not give up meeting together, as some are in the habit of doing, but let us encourage one another.'[6]

I realize that all this begs the question of what our particular church is like, but if it is to disciple people it may need to look again at what it offers in these areas. It is clear that a lot of what goes on in our churches does not serve the goal of discipleship training. As Robin Gamble somewhat succinctly put it, 'It has been rather painful writing a book called *The Irrelevant Church*. But then it has been painful belonging to an irrelevant church over the years.'[7]

23

WHAT HAVE THEY DONE TO THE WORLD?

The earth is the Lord's and all that is in it.

Psalm 24:1

Today we are all more environmentally aware. Recycling is big business and many of us feel guilty if we throw away things that could be used again. What kind of world we want to hand on to our children and our children's children is an important question. As Christians we do not have a great track record on environmental issues. Somebody once asked the penetrating question as to why the Church seemed to restrict its concern for conservation to liturgies, church buildings and churchyards. There didn't seem to be much to say in response!

One of the sadnesses of the past decade is that those who espouse a 'New Age' approach to spirituality seem to have taken the high ground on this particular subject. Indeed, many Christians seem to think that anything to do with the environment is immediately suspect. Yet surely this is a very big issue for the future of the human race on this planet. To avoid it because other people have 'got there first' is an abdication of our God-given responsibility. The title of this chapter is the serious question posed in a song written by songwriter and performer Michael Jackson, 'The Earth Song'. People have the feeling that our lack of apparent concern for the environment as Christians shows that there is something very deficient about our beliefs. The few Christians who do choose to make an issue of the environment and its care are viewed by others as cranks.

Yet surely our biblical heritage as Christians is very different. The early chapters of Genesis, some of the most important and most controversial chapters of the Bible, introduce us to a God who creates. We are told in Genesis that God created the world, that his creation was good and that this created world was handed to human beings to manage and to enjoy.[1] You would think that this was the perfect basis for Christians to take environmental issues seriously.

It is surely not a little eccentric for Christians in our urban and suburban areas to be decorating our churches as though they were rural churches at harvest thanksgiving and lustily singing hymns such as 'We plough the fields and scatter'! Harvest is a time of the year when we choose to thank God for his creation. Even though many of us no longer earn our living from the land, we still find some resonance with the harvest theme. The obvious question is, 'Why should this be?' What is it about this particular theme that excites our attention to the point where we are prepared to take part in such anachronistic activity?

Could it be that this theme evokes in us some subliminal need, a need to 'connect' with the creation of which we are but a part, a desire to connect with our Creator? It alarms me that many of those who have claimed the high ground of concern for the environment are apparently steeped in pagan religion. As Paul stated to the Christian congregation in Rome, speaking of the godless society in which the Church found itself, 'They exchanged the truth about God for a lie and worshipped and served the creature rather than the Creator.'[2] It seems a great shame that we Christians have all but surrendered care for the environment to those whose concern is based upon a lie.

The matter of the environment is crucial. Politicians know this, but often fear that environmental policies will cost too much and ultimately lose them a general election! The real dilemma is whether or not we can afford *not* to take such issues seriously. The subject is of particular importance to the young, for whom the environment has become a real concern. If as Christians we are to retain any credibility in today's world, this is an area in which we shall need to do better. It is surely a mystery, given our theology of creation, that our history of concern in this area is so inconsistent.

To care about the environment would have some challenging implications for Christians. It would mean we would need to distinguish between *saying* 'thank you' and *being* thankful. Our harvest thanksgiving is a classic example of this. We are encouraged at harvest to give thanks for what God has provided. This is not unimportant. In our childhood most of us had it drummed into us that saying 'thank you' was important. There is, however, as we well know, a huge difference between saying 'thank you' and being thankful. The plain fact is that we often find ourselves saying 'thank you' for things that we're not really very thankful for. Surely it could be said that people who are thankful show a greater evidence of being thankful than just saying 'thank you'. They might reciprocate by giving a gift themselves. They show their genuine gratitude by looking after what they have been given. They indicate their thankfulness by wanting to deepen their relationship with the giver.

It is evident that if, as a Church, our spirituality was more finely tuned to these issues, our impact would be greater. Merely saying 'thank you' is not enough. It is showing our thankfulness that will make a difference. What would such a change of heart look like?

First, it would mean taking a greater interest in sharing what we have. God has provided enough to feed the world. The problem is that some of us have too much, which means that by far the majority have too little. The pitiful images beamed into our comfortable sitting rooms of pathetic and malnourished children dying in the arms of their emaciated mothers have made us aware of the discrepancy in the distribution of the world's resources. Over a period of time we have also become anaesthetized to the tragedy of what we see. When it comes to generosity we can *all* do our bit. We can give of what we have. We can encourage our politicians to pursue just policies that will create a fairer sharing of the world's resources. The final straw is the destruction of 'food mountains' in the West whilst people starve in other parts of the world.

Second, we could exhibit our thankfulness by taking better care of what God has entrusted to us. It is no good our shying away from environmental issues on the basis that such matters are not for people like us. These are vital concerns and need to be addressed by Christians. For many of us becoming environmentally aware will mean embarking on a steep learning curve. We shall need to make adjustments to our lifestyle. We shall need to support those in politics who are willing to pursue openly Green policies. The crucial thing to remember is that we can all make a contribution to moving this agenda along.

Finally, we might wish to show our gratitude by deepening our relationship with the giver. In terms of the created world this means deepening our relationship with God. In a world where there is still a measure of respect and interest, especially amongst the young, for the wonder and intricacy of the created world, it may well be that a more accessible starting point for people's spiritual journey will be through issues such as those relating to the environment. This is not to lose sight of the full biblical picture of God as

Redeemer as well as Creator, but just to raise the question of where people are and therefore where they might begin.

Let me stress that people will read as much from our behaviour as our words. It will not be sufficient for us to be heard to say 'thank you'. We shall have to show that we are *being* thankful.

24

RELATING TO OTHERS

Two are better than one...

I remember a comic-strip cartoon I saw some years ago. The pictures told the story of a rather inadequate-looking man who had gone to a computer dating agency. Painstakingly he fed his personal details into the computer. The computer processed his input and then printed out the response: 'I love you!'

It does happen that some people find meaningful relationships, even a marriage partner, from a computer introduction. What is certain for us all is that our need for meaningful relationships is a very real one. Many individuals are deeply lonely; others are not only lonely, but bear the emotional scars of past, unsuccessful attempts to create good relationships.

As human beings we were made to be in relationship. The writer of the book of Genesis records that God decreed, 'It is not good that the man should be alone.'[1] We can find endless joy in our relationships, but we can also suffer immeasurable pain when they go wrong or end in an unresolved manner. Indeed, many of us are left so damaged as a result of bad relationships that we fear getting close to people again lest they let us down or reject us.

The Beatles song, 'All you need is love', expresses an important ingredient for a fulfilled life. The problem is where to find love. Some of us will go to extraordinary lengths to get it. But love can only function in a relationship, and that means that those who are trying to get love will also need to give it.

Jesus once met a woman from Samaria at a well.[2] Like a good number of people today she showed the mark of someone desperate to find love. Jesus, it seems, was able to identify her need as well as her fruitless search. He said to her, 'You are right in saying "I have no husband"; for you have had five husbands, and the one you have now is not your husband.'[3]

There is a very important question that needs to be asked. Can Jesus Christ offer anything to those who crave love? Can he bring any hope to those who have been damaged by past experiences? Can he inspire those who cannot give love, either because they do not know how to or because their need obscures their willingness to give?

In a world where there are a lot of hurting and lonely people these questions need to be addressed. At first sight such things would seem to be a long shot. Why would anyone think that a part-time carpenter/itinerant preacher, who lived in an obscure part of the Near East two thousand years ago, could bring good news to contemporary humanity? It is undoubtedly a very good question!

There are many Christians today, however, who would say that their faith in Christ has been of great assistance in helping them relate to others. To discover the love of God shown to us in Jesus is to open up the possibility of our being able to love others in a new way. One of the writers of the New Testament expressed this truth well when he wrote, 'In this is love, not that we loved God but that he loved us and sent his Son to be the atoning sacrifice for our sins. Beloved, since God loved us so much, we also ought to love one another.'[4]

Just as a plant will not develop properly unless it is exposed to light, so human beings become cases of arrested development if they are not exposed to love. Obviously, we don't all begin at the same starting point in this. Some of us find real love in our homes; some of us find the opposite. Some of us find our families accept us for who we are; many of us are left with the feeling that our acceptability is related to our achievement. Some, sadly, are the victims of abuse.

Are we to accept that some of us are damaged goods and that there is not much hope for us, or might there be a way in which a work of restoration could take place? Starting with that amazing story of the woman at the well, people have discovered that in meeting Jesus the process of transformation can begin. The New Testament gives numerous examples of this. And the same can happen today.

Sally,[5] an attractive woman in her thirties, was married to Jim, a high-achieving workaholic. On the outside their relationship looked fine, but within the marriage there was deep insecurity. Sally never felt secure. Because her parents had divorced she always feared that Jim would leave her and went to extreme lengths in her efforts to keep him. In an attempt to make herself feel and look good she would diet to excess, work out end-lessly at the gym and spend large amounts of money on the latest fashions. Her life was one long effort and became more and more pulled out of shape as her behaviour became more and more neurotic.

Jim, on the other hand, was a man who found it difficult to give love. He assumed that working hard and financing a comfortable lifestyle for his family would be interpreted by Sally and the children as caring behaviour. In fact the opposite was true; they felt increasingly neglected. The situation was compounded when Jim became friendly with another woman. She was younger, single and seemed to be more sympathetic. At first, Jim thought he could handle this friendship, but eventually and predictably the 'friendship' became adulterous. Sally discovered what was happening.

Sally had a good friend, Jill, who was a Christian. Sally herself wasn't over-interested in religion, although she had some fond memories of the chapel where as a child she had attended the Sunday school. Without being able to identify the reason, Sally always found Jill the kind of person to whom she could entrust personal problems. One evening Sally arrived at Jill's house broken-hearted by the discovery of Jim's affair. They talked late into the night. The following day Sally received from Jill a bunch of flow-ers and a card in which she had written, 'with love and prayers'. But Sally felt that her plight was beyond prayers!

Over the next weeks Jill spoke to Sally about God's love. Sally began to understand that her fears had given birth to neurotic behaviour. One evening, falteringly and in desperation, Sally became a new Christian. Initially she didn't feel much different, but little by little she began to emerge from the cocoon of fear that had shrouded her life. She began to feel that if the love of God was a forgiving love, then maybe she could begin to forgive Jim for his serious betrayal of trust. She said nothing to him of her new-found faith, but focused her efforts at home on a verse she had read in her New Testament. The verse read, 'This is my commandment, that you love one another as I have loved you.'[6]

Jim, who was guilt-ridden and working even harder than ever, had start-ed to drink in order to anaesthetize himself against the deep pain he felt. On his way home from work late one night he stopped his car in a lay-by and found himself doing something he had not done since he was a small boy. He wept like a baby. He even contemplated suicide.

There was something that struck Jim though. It was Sally. He couldn't quite work it out, but she was definitely different. Despite what he had done, she seemed committed to him. She had even told him she was trying to work out how to forgive him. She seemed less preoccupied with her 'image' and more preoccupied with other things. He couldn't understand it, but he began to grow in his admiration for her. One night he asked her what had happened to change her and then heard that she had found a faith in Jesus Christ. This was not an answer he would have anticipated. Although he was quite shocked at her response, he could not deny the amazing difference which was clearly evident to him.

To cut a long story short, largely because of the change he had seen in Sally, Jim also became a Christian and they now describe their marriage as 'born again'. There were, of course, tears along the road to recovery—they both had to look at some difficult things in their lives. But their story has been an inspiration to many and reiterates the truth that Jesus Christ can restore and rebuild broken relationships today.

The writer of the book of Ecclesiastes says 'two are better than one' and ends his piece on this matter with the words, 'A threefold cord is not quickly broken.'[7] The question for many people today is this: who will provide the third strand in your relationships?

25

FORGIVING OTHERS

Forgive us our sins, for we ourselves forgive everyone indebted to us.

Luke 11:4

It is three weeks before Remembrance Sunday. In today's newspaper is an article which tells of the outrage felt by some of the townspeople of Pembroke at the sight of a German Panzer division marching down the main street. They were there to mark the end of thirty-five years of German units training on Welsh firing ranges. Some World War II veterans were angered by what they saw and a local woman whose brother was killed during that war is quoted as saying: 'I never wanted to see them here in the first place. Young people today forget what we went through. Pembroke Dock was heavily bombed and four boys were lost from my street alone. I feel sick and betrayed and I know a lot of older people feel the same.'[1]

Clearly, for some of those people the soldiers' presence was an insult and an outrage, evoking memories of the horrors of war. For those not old enough to remember such times, the whole notion of 'remembrance' is a problem. Some clergy who have used Remembrance Sunday services to speak about reconciliation and forgiveness have found themselves criticized by those who can neither forgive nor forget. The article does, however, quote an eighty-one-year-old veteran of the Royal Tank Regiment, who saw many of his friends killed by Panzers in Normandy in 1944, as saying: 'I hated Germany and all things German for a long time after the war, but there's been a lot of water under the bridge since then. It's time to look to the future, not the past.'

One thing is evident from all this. *Forgiving others is a very difficult thing to do.*

At a more personal level we know that forgiving others is anything but easy. Part of our vulnerability as human beings is that we can be deeply hurt by the behaviour of others. Because of this many of us carry a huge amount of anger and resentment towards others through life.

It is equally clear that when we see unforgiveness in our world and in each other it is always an ugly thing to observe. Not a day goes by when, as we switch on the television or radio or open our newspapers, we are not reminded of the profoundly unattractive nature of deeply held anger and resentment targeted at others. At whatever level it takes place, be it an acrimonious divorce, or the kind of community tension we see in Northern Ireland or the former Yugoslavia, it is disturbing to witness and hard to see quite how in such circumstances forgiveness might occur. What is equally certain is that without some forgiveness in such situations there is little hope for the future.

Unforgiveness almost always leads to ongoing unhappiness. The New Testament implies that even within the Christian community, when unforgiveness is harboured in people's hearts it has a damaging impact upon their worship (Matthew 5:23), their prayer life (Mark 11:25), and even their ability to appropriate God's forgiveness (Luke 11:4). As Christians we should always take the initiative in putting things right—whether our brother or sister has something against us (Matthew 5:23), or whether we have something against our brother or sister (Matthew 18:15). One of the compelling facts about Jesus was that his behaviour always showed a willingness to step outside ethnic and gender prejudices (John 4:9) as well as social conventions (Luke 15:2).

Unforgiveness inhibits all relationships and should not be left unattended to. Whether it be in a marriage where infidelity has taken place, or where there are deep and historic community grievances, the inability to forgive can only bring further hurt to the parties concerned. Grudge-bearing is never a sound basis for harmonious relationships. Our problem is in knowing how to summon up the extra emotional resources to try and offer forgiveness to those who have either hurt us or someone we love. It is always alarming to hear someone say, 'I could never forgive them for what they have done.' But have we not all been guilty of such thoughts ourselves?

Jesus told a story about a king who was settling up with his slaves.[2] One of them owed him 10,000 talents. The slave pleaded with the king not to make him bankrupt; the king heard the slave's pleas and forgave him his debt. There is a 'sting in the tail' to this story, however. The slave to whom the king had shown mercy then came upon one of his fellow slaves who owed him a mere 100 denarii (a relatively insignificant sum) and demanded to be paid back, physically attacking him to add intimidation to his inflexibility. When the king discovered how the slave he had shown mercy to had treated his fellow slave, he was very angry and sent him to be tortured until such time as he had paid off his debt. The story concludes with these words: 'So my heavenly Father will also do to every one of you, if you do not forgive your brother or sister from your heart.'

At the heart of the Christian gospel there is forgiveness—the possibility that, in spite of our wrongdoing and selfishness, people like us can be forgiven. But with the offer and release of forgiveness there comes the challenge to be forgiving ourselves. The motivation to forgive is based on the fact that, although we do not deserve it, God in his grace forgives us when we come to him in repentance. There are people we shall come across in life who don't deserve our forgiveness either, but our responsibility as forgiven people ourselves is to be forgiving to others. Such teaching does not mean that it will suddenly become easy for us to forgive others. It is costly to forgive. No one knows that more than God himself who gave his Son on a cross for our forgiveness, 'for our sins'.[3]

The challenge of forgiveness is taken even further by Jesus in exhorting his followers to 'love your enemies'.[4] If we could all rise to that challenge what a very different place the world would become! When Gordon Wilson lost his daughter, Marie, in the IRA bombing incident at Enniskillen on Remembrance Day 1987, he had every right to allow his life to become shrouded in hatred and bitterness. But he didn't. His message to the bombers was one of forgiveness. Such forgiveness is certainly not something we can easily imagine: put in his place most of us would expect to be torn apart by anger and profound resentment. In spite of his terrible grief and torment, however, Gordon Wilson forgave in the belief that God had forgiven him and called upon him to forgive others.

Forgiveness is a key that could unlock many different situations. I believe it is very doubtful that real healing can take place between dissenting individuals or communities without the forgiveness factor—the one thing that can break into the circles of hatred and violence. Without it the cycle just goes on and on.

If we wait until others deserve our forgiveness, we shall have a very long wait. It is salutary to remind ourselves that if God had waited until we deserved his forgiveness, he would have had an endless wait on his hands!

Our usual instinct is to delay any attempt at reconciliation with those we believe have wronged us; we tell ourselves that we will wait until we are ready. But so often 'tomorrow never comes'.

I once worked in a factory and I remember a middle-aged lady who was an assistant supervisor there. She was highly thought of, both by the girls in her department and the factory management. Quite suddenly and without obvious reason she became a poor time keeper and was absent from work on a regular basis, although never more than a day or so at time, which meant she was not required to bring a doctor's sick note explaining what was wrong with her. All of us began to talk behind her back, criticizing her apparent laziness. When she did show up for work she was always withdrawn and this led us to criticize her further, believing her to be uninterested in us.

One day I was asked by the works manager to make a visit to her home and find out what was going on. Although nothing was said directly, the aim was to sack the woman. I arrived at the house and her husband came to the door. To my horror he told me his wife was suffering from a serious cancer and was too unwell that day to see anyone. We had all judged her too hastily. None of us ever got the chance to say we were sorry and to ask for her forgiveness, for that night she died.

If we wait until we are ready, we might never have the opportunity to put things right. If we try to forgive in our own strength, we will never be strong enough for the task. If we ourselves have a genuine sense of having been forgiven, even though we have not deserved it, then we may find both the inspiration and the motivation to offer forgiveness to others.

The apostle Paul, when writing to the Christians in Colossae, encouraged them with these words: 'Forgive each other just as the Lord has forgiven you.'[5] Such a prescription could offer real healing to us and our conflict-torn world in which we live and for which Jesus died.

26

FORGIVING MYSELF

**Have mercy on me, O God, according to your steadfast
love... For I know my transgressions, and my sin is ever
before me.**

Psalm 51:1, 3

There is a true story of a man who, several years ago, had a heated
exchange with his wife and stormed out of the house in a mood. He jumped
into his car and reversed at high speed out of the garage. He had not
noticed his two-year-old daughter in the driveway. The car knocked her
down and killed her. I remember hearing at the time of the tragedy that the
distraught man asked the question that I suspect many of us ask ourselves:
'How can I ever forgive myself?'

Over the years I have met many people who have come to terms with
being able to appropriate God's forgiveness. I have come across others who
have found the necessary strength to forgive those who at some stage have
badly hurt them. It is also my experience that many of us find it difficult to
forgive ourselves. Such a legacy of this kind of unforgiveness is often related to behaviour that was totally unintended, such as the example given
above where the outcome was neither intended nor predicted.

I knew a single lady who had made major personal sacrifices in order to
care for her elderly, sick and, truthfully, rather unpleasant mother. Towards
the very end of the mother's life the level of nursing care she required was
far more than her daughter could reasonably provide. Consequently, when
a hospital bed became available the daughter gladly accepted it, although
her mother did not want it. The mother died in hospital and the years
following her death were marked by depression in her daughter. She
repeatedly said to me, 'I just can't forgive myself for allowing Mum to die in
hospital.'

At one level such feelings are irrational. It was pointed out that over all
the years the daughter's care had been exemplary, that the mother's need

was so great towards the end of her life that it was better met by professionals. All such reassurance was to no avail. The daughter continued to punish herself for what she construed to be her own failure.

Reflecting on all this you begin to see that part of our complexity as human beings is that we never actually 'forgive and forget' big things in our lives. Part of our problem is that unlike the computers that have become part and parcel of our lives we cannot erase our memories at the press of a button.

Thankfully God is able to forgive and forget. The psalmist asks God to 'blot out' his transgressions and to 'wash me thoroughly from my iniquity'.[1] To coin a phrase, God can 'wipe the slate clean'. The trouble is that we cannot and we thereby become victims of guilt over very prolonged periods. Some of us, when we get into the long-term personal guilt trip, begin to fit situations and occurrences into a picture which reinforces our sense of guilt. For instance, people who feel personal guilt for past wrongs tend to see subsequent difficulties in life as part of the process of ongoing punishment for their previous wrongdoing. In a recent newspaper article Rick Parfitt, forty-eight-year-old guitarist with rock band Status Quo, is quoted as saying, following the death by drowning of his two-year-old daughter, Heidi: 'I hate to think it was my fault, but in a way I think maybe it was. My fault for being the way I was. This was my punishment.'[2]

We can quickly see that part of the problem is our need to continue to punish ourselves. It may seem almost masochistic, but I think a lot of people have a need to inflict chastisement on themselves for things that they have done wrong in their lives, be they intentional or not. Is there any way we can learn to deal with this? The world tells us that 'time heals all things', and there is certainly some truth in this. Given time, our adaptability as human beings means that we can learn to live 'around' our guilt and our propensity not to forgive ourselves.

At one level there is a fundamental question to be answered. If the God who made the heavens and the earth and all that dwells within can forgive us, what is it that makes us so unwilling to forgive ourselves? I suspect that we shall have a hope of forgiving ourselves only if we have the sure knowledge that God has forgiven us. Of course, the route to self-forgiveness is inhibited when another party refuses to forgive us. Sometimes our ability to forgive ourselves will depend on working to restore a relationship with another person.

At this point it is worth noting that one of the New Testament angles on the death of Christ is that which makes the staggering claim that Christ bore the punishment for our sins upon the cross,[3] that there is a substitutionary element to his death. In turning to Christ we become recipients of the benefit of his death, in that we are released from the consequences of our wrongdoing because the punishment has already been carried out.

The writer of the Epistle to the Hebrews, in comparing the death of Jesus with the sacrificial system of the Jews, says, 'How much more will the blood of Christ, who through the eternal Spirit offered himself without blemish to God, purify our conscience from dead works to worship the living God.'[4] The antidote to a mindset that tells us we can't forgive ourselves is surely a purified conscience. How will we get a purified conscience? By trusting that the consequences of our sin have already been dealt with in Jesus upon the cross.

The access point for that kind of releasing forgiveness is repentance. Repentance does not mean just saying 'sorry'; it also carries the idea of turning away from our wrongdoing and turning to Christ in whom our forgiveness is wrought. It marks a change of life, a change of attitude.

There is little doubt that we shall only start to forgive ourselves when we reach that point when we are ready to let go and stop punishing ourselves. There is something about the element of choice here. To a certain extent we can choose to continue to punish ourselves or we can choose to stop. The fact that there is no need for us to continue with self-punishment because of what God in Christ has done for us is an encouragement to us all.

The knowledge that certain things that happen in life are our fault poses a real threat to our well-being. That tragic case of the man who killed his own daughter is a reminder that we are fallible creatures. Those of us who drive are aware that we all make mistakes. Almost all the time we get away with our errors, but there are unfortunately some of us who don't and then damage, injury and even death can ensue.

Learning to live with our fallibility is important. Though we are 'fearfully and wonderfully made',[5] we are also capable of making mistakes. That fact alone can be potentially annihilating. It is only when we can counterbalance our frailty with the confidence of knowing that he who made us will always forgive us when we turn to him, that we are able to face the riskiness of life. Although there are some words and actions we shall never forget, the reality of God's forgiveness can give us a new perspective from which we can learn to live peacefully with them.

27

FORGIVING GOD?

When disaster brings sudden death, he mocks at the calamity of the innocent.

Job 9:23

Some years ago when my family and I were on holiday in Wales we came upon a magnificent castle with a beautiful river flowing past it. The day was hot and sunny and as we had our swimsuits with us we were able to spend a very happy couple of hours swimming in the river. As we enjoyed it so much we returned a couple of days later to swim again, but whilst changing into our swimming things we were approached by a man walking his dog along the river bank who warned us not to swim there. He told us that during the previous summer two boys had dived into the river. Beneath the appealing surface of the water were the twisted roots of the trees that lined the river bank. The boys had become trapped in those roots and had drowned.

That tragic happening reminded me that on the surface many of us appear smooth and attractive. Beneath the surface, however, we can be a mass of twisted emotions and hurts. When it comes to people, 'what you see' is not always 'what you get'. In our churches there are many who are like that. Week by week they sit in church, seemingly supportive of what is going on, but within them there is anger. If the truth were known they would probably admit that they were angry with God. The reasons for this will be many, but the possibility is there for us all.

There will be times in our lives when believing in the goodness of God will be a demanding thing. I know this for myself. There are times when we are all tested in this, but when anger and resentment are our long-term feelings towards God, then we need help. I have met widowers and widows who have built up anger with God because they cannot come to terms with 'why he took away my wife/husband'. Similarly, coming to terms with the death of a child or someone whom we think of as too young to die can agitate feelings of bitterness. This century the Holocaust stands as a grim reminder of the terrible things human beings do to each other and still raises a good deal of anger in people as to why such things are 'allowed' to happen.

John Stott recounts a story from a concentration camp in World War II. A group of learned Jews in Buchenwald decided to put God on trial for neglecting his chosen people. Witnesses appeared for the prosecution and defence and the judges were rabbis. They found God guilty and solemnly condemned him.[1] Although such a trial is indeed shocking, it is understandable and a frank reminder that feelings of anger towards God are possible within all of us.

Does it matter? Does it matter that there are, I suspect, an appreciable number of people going through life feeling angry with God? Clearly it does. Such feelings betray bitterness. People who harbour such bitterness are rarely fulfilled and are often disgruntled about a lot of things. Few people actually enjoy the experience of feeling angry. It is also probable that such anger will stand in the way of a relationship with God. Just as anger is a limiting factor in human relationships, the same is true of our relationship with God.

Because we don't know what to do with our anger we tend to bury it within. All this means is that we carry it with us. It is strange that we are prepared to do this, but anger is such a frightening emotion to face up to, either in ourselves or in others, that it should come as no surprise that we attempt to hide it away.

The Bible is less reticent to talk about such anger. Indeed, it is because of anger that Jesus ended up on the cross. The crowd that on Palm Sunday cheered Jesus into Jerusalem was no doubt the same crowd which just a few days later shouted, 'Crucify him.' The ugliness and destructive power of anger resulted in Jesus on the cross.

There are other instances of people who became angry with God. Jonah, we are told, was displeased with God and became angry with him.[2] For what reason? Because Jonah felt that God had let him down, because his expectations of what God would do to the people of Nineveh came to nothing. It occurs to me that this is often our problem. Like that crowd in Jerusalem, we can be angry when we feel that our expectations have not been met. But is there any way in which we might be able to deal with this anger, or are we left simply to reap its consequences?

An appropriate question that arises is, how might we properly express our anger within the acceptable limits of our culture? The answer is by no means clear. Obviously, out-of-control rage is not acceptable, but neither is burying our anger within. Expressing our anger to God seems even more complicated, not least within our churches where people are preoccupied with being 'nice' to each other.

Within the Old Testament the concept of being angry with God and expressing that vexation is not such a foreign idea. When Jonah was mad with God, he told him in no uncertain terms. God listened to him and then invited him to check out his anger.[3] The psalmist found himself frustrated and let down by God.[4] At first sight it looks as though even if we cannot cope with our anger, God can! Expressing it can be the beginning of our healing. I have often wondered why amongst our many liturgies we don't have one designed to help us deal with our anger.

The starting point may well be for us to be honest about this. I believe many people would be tempted to deny anger focused on God. The likelihood is that such anger, if unexpressed, will be subject to transference, that is, it will manifest itself somewhere else in our lives.

Our anger is, of course, made harder to deal with because God appears to be indifferent to it. But is God as indifferent as he seems? Surely the cross of Christ is a concrete reminder that God is not actually indifferent to human suffering, but has immersed himself in it on Calvary. The issue of whether God is impassible (Latin *impassibilis*, meaning incapable of suffering) was a Greek notion that was somewhat uncritically adopted by the Early Fathers of the Church. But surely the God whose Son ended up on a cross is not incapable of suffering? William Temple on this subject thought that the term 'impassible', as used by most theologians to mean 'incapable of suffering', was, when attributed to God, almost wholly false.[5]

Helping people to own their anger in this respect is an entirely positive thing. Assisting people in understanding that God can cope with our anger is crucial. Pointing to the cross as the evidence for the love of God and the suffering of God is the place where our healing can begin.

Two or three years ago I was invited to give a Lenten lecture on forgiveness at a prestigious Roman Catholic abbey. In preparing for the talk I covered the usual areas: 'receiving God's forgiveness', 'forgiving others' and 'forgiving myself'. It was during this time of preparation that I suddenly became aware that perhaps an area of forgiveness we seldom address is 'forgiving God'. I struggled over whether to speak about this, but decided that I would prepare a short section under that heading and, if it seemed appropriate, I would use it. On the night there were a number of mostly elderly Christian men and women gathered and in the end I did speak to them about 'forgiving God'. The effect was unexpected.

There were tears and there was healing. I remember a woman who had lost a child, probably forty or more years ago, thanking me with tear-filled eyes because she had discovered a new context for her feeling, and a man whose experiences of World War II had left him with a lot of unresolved emotion finding a new way of expressing it.

I don't think I shall ever forget that evening, even though I find it difficult to explain and describe what I witnessed. I do know that I came away believing that this is a very important subject, and that just because it feels unsafe it cannot be disregarded.

In the passage from the book of Job which heads this chapter, Job in the depths of his personal suffering expresses his feeling that 'he [God] mocks at the calamity of the innocent'.[6] Such a thought has crossed the mind of every honest person who has known what it is to suffer. Our anger is often justified. The real challenge, however, is whether that anger can be transformed.

28

WISE UP!

**The fear of the Lord is the beginning of all knowledge;
fools despise wisdom and instruction.**

Proverbs 1:7

Life today is about making decisions. Almost hourly they have to be made about one thing or another. A good many of them are trivial and even if we made a 'bad call' it wouldn't really matter that much. But what about life's important decisions—the hard ones we face which may make a profound difference to how we will experience life? Where will we get help with such decisions?

In a consumer society choice is worshipped as a fundamental human option. Indeed, in recent years it has almost become a fundamental human right. This week in Parliament, the British prime minister, accompanied by loud 'hear, hear's, declared, 'I believe in choice.' That human beings are able to make choices is indeed a privilege. But such a privilege brings with it the responsibility to choose wisely. The choices we make are rarely made in a vacuum and the outcome of many of them also has an effect on the lives of others.

A large number of cultures hold the attribute of wisdom in high esteem. Within our own culture, wisdom is viewed as a positive characteristic. We feel we are complimenting another person if we describe them as 'wise'. But what is wisdom? How can it be acquired? What kind of difference would it make to my life? These are not unimportant questions, for it is undoubtedly true that we connect the ability to make right decisions with wisdom.

An immediate assumption we make is that age and wisdom go hand in hand, believing that wisdom is something we 'pick up' as we go through life. There is, of course, something in this. The New Testament word for 'leader' is a Greek word that can be translated as 'elder'. This is not some kind of semantic accident, but rather a recognition that the kind of wisdom required for leadership in a church was likely to be allied to experience of life. However, it is true that there are some younger people who exhibit sound and mature judgment. Timothy, a New Testament church leader, was young.[1] Today, we speak of some individuals as having 'an old head on young shoulders'.

The Bible speaks a good deal about wisdom. Interestingly, Old Testament books such as Proverbs and Ecclesiastes are viewed by many Christians today as somewhat marginal contributions to the Bible. The danger is that if we see wisdom as purely an Old Testament concept, we forget that the theme of wisdom is prevalent in the New Testament. One of the well-known stories told by Jesus draws the distinction between the wise and the foolish. It is noteworthy that the comparison made in scripture is between the 'wise' and the 'foolish', rather than the 'wise' and the 'not-so-wise'.

'Everyone then who hears these words of mine and acts on them will be like a wise man who built his house on a rock. The rain fell, the floods came, and the winds blew and beat on that house, but it did not fall, because it had been founded on rock. And everyone who hears these words of mine and does not act on them will be like a foolish man who built his house on sand. The rain fell, and the floods came, and the winds blew and beat against that house, and it fell—and great was its fall!'[2]

We live in a world where there is an impressive amount of intelligence. The knowledge and brilliance of many twentieth-century minds is awesome. Even so, we might well question whether there is enough wisdom around. To be wise is to have knowledge, but it is more than that. Wisdom offers the ability not merely to describe, but to prescribe. Wisdom adds a quality to the lives of individuals and communities that nothing else can bring. A well-known motor manufacturing company advertises its vehicles as 'greater than the sum of their parts'. That phrase captures something of the spirit of wisdom.

Individuals have a need for wisdom. Communities need to access wise thinking. Even nations require wise government. T.S. Eliot in his poem 'The Rock' laments our loss in this area:

Where is the life we have lost in living?
Where is the wisdom we have lost in knowledge?
Where is the knowledge we have lost in information?[3]

In a world which adulates choice, the need for wisdom is surely even greater. Its impact is always positive and never destructive.

But, what is wisdom? How are we to distinguish between true wisdom and false wisdom? How can we tell what is wholesome and true and what is superficial and based in half-truth? These are significant questions, not least in a society which seems to have an ideological, cultural and spiritual void at its centre. Fifty years ago people would have looked to clergy for wisdom and guidance, but this is less likely to happen today.

Writing in the New Testament, James offers some very upfront advice to Christians who were struggling to exist in the face of persecution:

If any of you is lacking in wisdom, ask God, who gives to all generously and ungrudgingly, and it will be given you. But ask in faith, never doubting, for the one who doubts is like a wave of the sea, driven and tossed by the wind. [4]

In other words, the biblical witness seems to place huge store on wisdom being associated with trusting God. That wisdom becomes almost a by-product of trusting God, though in truth it is a very important and necessary by-product. The writer of the book of Proverbs in the Old Testament makes a similar point:

The fear of the Lord is the beginning of knowledge; fools despise wisdom and instruction. [5]

Putting the biblical witness together it could be summarized as follows: if we want wisdom we are to ask God for it, in faith. God gives his Holy Spirit to those who trust him and that Spirit helps us understand God's word (the Bible) which was 'inspired' by that same Spirit. Trust in God and instruction in God's word are therefore indispensable factors in gaining wisdom. Such a view of wisdom releases it from the constraints of age, gender, educational background and IQ. It is indeed possible to be both simple and wise.

What would wisdom look like? Thinking about this is extremely challenging. What marks wisdom from any other advice? How might we recognize it? The following is offered not as an exhaustive list of attributes of wisdom, but to try to give a feel for what it looks like:

Wisdom:	The foolish person:
• always pauses and listens.	• reacts in a moment.
• is concerned with outcomes.	• is consumed with process alone.
• tells me what I need to know.	• is *only* concerned to tell me what he/she knows.
• pays attention to relationships.	• sees people as a means to an end.
• has time.	• is on overload.
• gives advice that builds up the hearer.	• merely tells other people what to do.
• can appreciate shades of grey.	• sees only black and white.

The possibility that all of us might access wisdom is surely an encouragement. Sensible people realize their need for guidance (we'll be exploring that further in the next chapter). Significantly, people are always attracted by wisdom, even if they don't necessarily like what they hear. This is partly because wise people are able to communicate their wisdom in a way which is neither bullying nor offensive. The relationship between wisdom and faith in God is crucial. From speaking to businesspeople throughout the world, it is clear to me that wisdom is a commodity which is recognized as fundamental. There is also the realization that it is in short supply! Abba Eban, giving a speech in London in December 1970, said, 'History teaches us that men and nations behave wisely once they have exhausted all other alternatives.'[6]

Human history has, to some extent, been the story of the interface of wisdom and foolhardiness.

The following prayer is attributed to Reinhold Niebuhr:

God give us the serenity to accept what cannot be changed;
Give us the courage to change what should be changed;
Give us the wisdom to distinguish one from the other.[7]

29

GIVING AND RECEIVING

It is more blessed to give than to receive.

Acts 20:35

A famous, if apocryphal, misprint appeared in a parish magazine. An article on Christian giving was meant to begin with a text from 2 Corinthians, 'God loves a cheerful giver.'[1] Unfortunately, the proof-reader failed to notice a typographical error and the text actually read, 'God loves a cheerful fiver'!

The issue to be addressed in this chapter is not so much what we do with our wallets, but what we do with our hearts. There is a profound paradox found throughout the New Testament: we are asked to be generous in spirit—to be 'giving' people—with the assurance that generosity will bring blessing, but at the same time the promise of blessing is not to be regarded as an incentive to being generous, that is, our generosity should not be influenced by a desire to achieve personal gain.

This is in sharp contrast to the way the world thinks. At the heart of commerce is the concept of investing in order to receive back the highest interest. Our consumerist world is always in danger of totally rejecting the whole idea of selfless generosity. Charities are well aware that they will attract more financial support if they offer the public a return or incentive for their giving, thus courting the idea of 'giving to receive'. In consequence, charity dinners, for which tickets are sold at exorbitant prices, are the order of the day. These occasions will often include an auction, allowing those present to parade their wealth by trying to outbid each other for relatively mundane items. The 'charity shop' is another example of 'paying your money and getting your goods'. By comparison, the volunteer shaking the tin outside the supermarket on a Saturday morning represents a far less effective means of fund-raising, for all that is given in return for a contribution is a self-adhesive label!

Big charity occasions are often great fun and charity shops certainly have their place in providing bargains. The point, however, is this. Nowadays decreasing attention is given to genuine giving. Not only is this true in respect of material giving, it is also evident in other areas of life.

In relationships, for instance, much emphasis is placed upon 'give and take'. As is the case with many half-truths, there is something important here for us to grasp, although there is real danger also. Anyone who has been in any kind of relationship for any duration recognizes that there are times when the only hope for the long-term well-being of the relationship is to give without the expectation of receiving anything in return. The practice of only giving to others if they are likely to reciprocate has little hope of leading to long-term relationships with any degree of mutual fulfilment. Such emotional table tennis is unlikely to sustain a lasting relationship. But in almost any context of society today we find it particularly difficult to separate the concept of giving from the outcome of receiving. It has to be added that selfless generosity does not often come naturally to us and it is therefore difficult for us to fathom. For most of us, self-giving is, I contend, the result of lengthy and often painful personal development.

Paul describes Jesus as having once said, 'It is more blessed to give than to receive.'[2] Today's culture easily dismisses this kind of talk. In our lottery age, where so many are hopeful of receiving enormous amounts, such teaching is easily and readily marginalized. We need to understand that the impact of consumerism is far wider than our attitude to our possessions alone. It affects the whole of our lives. We are in great danger of seeing people as things. There is no need to have a very vivid imagination to work out that when we begin to see people as objects, we very soon start to treat them as such. As soon as they have outlived their usefulness to us, we trade them in for someone new. A brief look at our society reveals ample evidence of this.

The principle that to give is more blessed than to receive seems like a long shot for the kind of society that most of us live in. Does all this greed and emphasis upon self result in a society that is whole? The evidence would appear to prove otherwise. Quite recently a public debate on morality has been promoted in the media, and even though much of the discussion focuses on tackling the symptoms rather than the causes, it is a debate to be welcomed.

It is worth asking why Jesus would promote such an apparently odd idea as it is more blessed to give than to receive. Is there something here we should think about more carefully? Might there be a joy in giving, both of ourselves and of what we have, which needs to be closely scrutinized in a world where self-interest is consistently placed at the front of the queue and self-denial jostled to the back?

At the same time we must ask ourselves whether our churches have promoted the value of self-denial, or whether the spirit of the age has begun to infect the way those churches think and behave. On reflection, many of our churches, particularly those where there is growth and life, may be guilty of sending out a contrary message. The priority given to receiving health, healing, prosperity, wholeness, and so on is only a part of the story. If we choose to nurture Christians to understand their faith *only* in terms of what they can get out of it, they will never understand that fundamental aspect of Christianity that our Lord designated as self-denial.

The integrity of Jesus' teaching lies in the fact that he himself modelled what he taught. The phrase 'It is more blessed to give than to receive' was not just a neat slogan designed to be a 'show-stopper' amongst the crowds that Jesus taught. It was something that mattered to him. Indeed, it mattered enough for him to give his life. Jesus was a supreme example of self-giving love. In a world dominated by self-assertion, Jesus has shown us that there is an alternative.

In Philippians, Paul meditates on the very nature of Jesus' sacrifice:

Though he was in the form of God,
[he] did not regard equality with God
as something to be exploited,
but emptied himself,
taking the form of a slave,
being born in human likeness.
And being found in human form,
he humbled himself
and became obedient to the point of death—
even death on a cross.[3]

The question now before us is, how will our hearts be moved to generosity? The fact that Jesus provides an excellent example for us is probably not enough to bring about the change of heart that will lead us to self-giving love. Such a change will have to come from within, and this is where God can help us. When we come to trust in Jesus, the Bible promises that God empowers us in a new way, with his Holy Spirit who comes to dwell within us. Paul wrote in his letter to the Ephesians, 'In him you also, when you had heard the word of truth, the gospel of your salvation, and had believed in him, were marked with the seal of the promised Holy Spirit.'[4]

God's Spirit within us can work that miracle of inner transformation, helping us to become more Christ-like in our behaviour. Paul goes on to describe the authenticating mark of the Spirit's presence in our lives as 'fruit', that is, what is 'grown' in the lives of God's faithful people. In Galatians chapter 5, Paul gives examples of the kind of qualities that would constitute 'fruit' in the life of the believer. He says, 'The fruit of the Spirit is love, joy, peace, patience, kindness, generosity, faithfulness, gentleness, and self control.'[5] It is a by-product of consumerism that in our churches we much more readily focus upon the 'gifts' of the Spirit, whilst relegating the 'fruit' to the occasional uncomfortable sermon or home group.

Charles[6] was a very successful commodities dealer. He had considerable personal wealth, a beautiful home and, frankly, could buy just about anything he wanted. At the start of his successful career, however, his wealth did not bring him the pleasure he had anticipated. Like many gifted businesspeople, he had a mean streak within him. On his own admission, his stinginess was such that he would not even give a few pence to homeless people on the street. Eventually, through his dissatisfaction with wealth and through the gentle witness of his wife, he made the decision to become a Christian. Since that time the Holy Spirit has been quietly working within Charles, challenging some of his deeply held insecurities. Today he is able to give away 75 per cent of his income, and, significantly, has discovered that he enjoys the remaining 25 per cent in a new way. What is even more notable is that those who know Charles can see that his new generosity is not just related to the sharing of his material wealth. They would say he is 'more giving' as a human being within his relationships.

Examples like this are encouraging. It is not implied, however, that such transformation is easy. The Holy Spirit's work is often a deeply painful and costly process, as radical surgery usually is. But the outcome is a new way of looking at life; a way that will help us, albeit gradually, to begin to glimpse the reality of what Jesus was talking about when he said, 'It is more blessed to give than to receive.'

An old verse sets the generosity that God looks for in us within the context of his amazing graciousness:

'What, giving again?' I asked in dismay,
'and must I keep giving and giving alway?'
'Oh no,' said the angel, whose gaze pierced me through,
'Just stop when the Saviour stops giving to you!'

30

OPTIONS FOR CHANGE

Cast all your anxiety on him, because he cares for you.

1 Peter 5:7

It is said that as two tourists left Windsor Castle one of them was heard to say to his companion, 'What a wonderful castle, it was everything I had read about in the guidebooks and more.' His friend replied, 'It sure is wonderful, but why did the Queen build it so near to the airport?'

It is widely thought, and with good reason, that if you lose a sense of history you lose something important. A plausible reason offered for the serious study of history is to avoid making the mistakes of the past. It would be good to think this was so. However, I recently heard a moral philosopher remark somewhat cynically that, 'the lesson of history is that there is no lesson'. In other words, we human beings find it very difficult to learn from our past mistakes. Whether we are talking about whole communities or individuals, it appears to be self-evident. Why is it that we find it so difficult *not* to repeat yesterday's mistakes? Why do we find it so hard to change ourselves?

There is little doubt that we have been heavily influenced by the thinking and the language of modern psychology. The findings of men like Jung, Freud, Maslow and Rogers have had quite an impact upon the way we look at ourselves. Although most of us have never read their writings, there is a sense in which we have all 'bought' something of their message and allowed it to become deeply embedded in our thinking. *It is clear that we now readily accept that our past affects what we are in the present.* Indeed, we are inclined to see ourselves very much as the product of our past experiences.

This is an important insight and its truth is self-apparent. Those of us who are parents are aware that the way we treat our children will affect the way they will grow up. Such awareness has probably influenced the way we parent our children. Most of us know that in travelling along life's highways we have picked up a few 'dents'. Although we are reluctant to admit this in ourselves we are more than ready to see it in others. Does it matter?

Michel Quoist wrote, 'Unless you make your feelings, your remorse and your regret things of the past, they can effectively cripple your personal life.'[1] It is clear that many of us are captives of our past in a very negative way:

- Maybe it is something we have done in the past that we find difficult to live with in the present
- Maybe it is something that someone has done to us
- Maybe disaster and trauma have hit us out of nowhere with devastating effect

Is there any hope of change for people like us?

A popular local venue at weekends is the waste tip. All day long people arrive with their car boots or trailers overladen with things to throw away. The mood of these people is generally convivial. They talk to one another in a way they probably would not when meeting strangers in a different setting. It is as if the act of throwing things away helps people feel better about themselves. I have often thought how great it would be if there were such a place as a rubbish tip for our unwanted emotional refuse, somewhere to dump our personal 'rubbish'. There is a sense in which the Bible offers us a means of doing this, for the good news is that we can bring all our rubbish to Jesus.

The apostle Peter invited his readers to, 'Cast all your anxiety on him [Jesus], because he cares for you.'[2] For some the idea of enlisting God's help is quaint, for others the very thought of God evokes fear, guilt, anger and cynicism. But that should not deter us from presenting people with the choice. They can either choose to hold on to their negative feelings from the past, or they can choose to explore the option of help from God.

Incidentally, to explore the option of seeking God's help does not preclude the possibility of seeking help from others. There are those whose Christianity has led them to what is undoubtedly an extreme position, that is, their belief that to consider an option other than that of trusting God is in itself a lack of faith. They would strongly discourage anyone from seeking help other than from God. They might even suggest that a person should not take prescribed medication. To imply that seeking help from professionals or taking prescribed medication is a lack of faith is undoubtedly wrong, for surely we need to understand that God is able to work through all of this. Most of us would conclude that if we developed acute appendicitis we would ask our friends to pray for us, but at the same time would plan to get to hospital as soon as we possibly could!

Because we are dealing today with people who are consumers, we need not be afraid to put to them the *choice* to trust God. They are likely to be more engaged by a 'what if' rather than a 'this is it' approach. 'What if there were a way to deal with my past?' rather than the 'I found Jesus and all my problems were solved' kind of approach. Putting options before people is an important part of contending for the Christian faith and often helps us to get to the real obstacles people have in trusting God.

Lee Strobel was a journalist, the legal affairs correspondent on the *Chicago Tribune*. He was also an atheist. Lesley, his wife, had become a Christian and Lee was intrigued by the change he saw in her. He couldn't easily explain it. To please his wife he started attending a church where the option to trust God was consistently put before those present. Although the possibility for such life-change was so frequently put forward, Lee found that the church also allowed him the space to come to his own decision. This was done in such a way that Lee could relate the messages he heard to his own life. Eventually, Lee hesitantly prayed this prayer: 'God, I don't believe you're there, but if you are I want to find you. I really *do* want to know the truth, so if you exist please show yourself to me.'[3] What a great prayer! Into the apparently unpromising atheistic soil of Lee's life a seed of faith had been sown. He did the only thing that he could if he was to maintain his integrity. He asked God to pour some water on that seed, and slowly the seed began to grow. Lee is now a pastor at the church!

The Bible suggests that there is only one way that we can know God, and that is through his Son, Jesus Christ. Jesus said, 'I am the way, and the truth, and the life. No one comes to the Father except through me.'[4] The overwhelming evidence of the New Testament is that those who trusted God through Christ were able to make a new start. People who were victims of their past were set free to try again.[5] People who were held captive by long illnesses on occasions found healing.[6]

A woman who had recently found a faith in God was enthusing at her home group about the difference it had make to her life. In her attempt to describe the fresh start she had received through Christ she declared, 'It's like... I can hardly describe it ... it's like being born again.' I think I've heard that somewhere before!

EPILOGUE: WHEN 5 + 2 + 1 = 5,000

Taking the five loaves...

Mark 6:41

The purpose of this book is to help you to make a difference as a Christian. It may well be that these chapters have set you thinking about your faith in new and creative ways. It is possible that you may feel just a little more confident about adding some 'salt' to conversations that occur beyond the comfort zone of our church communities. My starting point in all these chapters has been the Word of God and its profound relevance to life as we experience it. It is written from the conviction that the written Word of God (the Bible) always leads us to the Living Word of God (Jesus).

Thinking about the somewhat marginal position of the Church in society today, it is easy to be daunted by the task before we begin. I imagine that when the disciples of Jesus were faced with a crowd of 5,000 hungry people to feed, they were similarly daunted. They were in a lonely place with no money. There was just a lad with five loaves and two fishes, and Jesus. It was hardly enough for a decent family picnic!

When the disciples gave to Jesus the small amount of food the boy had brought, something happened—and a multitude was fed. The story goes on to tell us that twelve baskets of scraps were collected at the end. In this matter of contending for the Christian faith we can learn something important. If we wait until we are ready, we shall never begin. But if we do start out, offering the little we have, we shall soon discover that it can be used by God to go a very long way.

I hope that you will feel encouraged and energized to undertake the task that God has called us to—to be witnesses. Offer what you have to Jesus and I think you, with those disciples of old, will be astounded by the results.

NOTES

Introduction
1. Robert Warren, *Signs of Life—How goes the Decade of Evangelism?*, Church House Publishing, 1996, page 49
2. 1 Peter 3:15
3. Donald Posterski, *Re-inventing Evangelism*, IVP (USA), 1989, page 31

Chapter 1
1. Mark 8:38
2. Ruth Etchells, *Set my People Free*, Fount, 1995, pages 14–15
3. Matthew 28:19
4. John 20:21
5. Acts 1:8
6. Acts 4:31
7. Hebrews 9:27
8. Acts 16:30
9. Ephesians 2:8 (NIV)
10. Romans 6:23
11. David Watson, *I Believe in the Church*, Hodder and Stoughton, 1978, pages 180–81

Chapter 2
1. *Daily Telegraph Weekend Magazine*, 19 October 1996, page 4
2. Vasso Kortesis, *The Duchess of York*, Blake, 1996
3. Bertrand Russell, 'Outline of Intellectual Rubbish', from *Unpopular Essays*, 1950
4. Psalm 14:1
5. John 11:25
6. Luke 6:43–44

Chapter 3
1. Romans 7:18–19
2. 1 John 1:9
3. Matthew 4:1–11; Luke 4:1–13
4. Hebrews 4:16

Chapter 4

1. I use the term 'unchurched' throughout the book on the grounds that it better describes the paradox that lies at the heart of our nation. Namely, that whenever polls are carried out asking about beliefs, it is usual to discover that 70 per cent of people claim belief in God and roughly the same percentage claim to have had 'religious experience'. At the same time, only about 10 per cent of the population express that commitment through regular attendance at church. The term 'unchurched' seems a reasonable way of describing the phenomenon of 'believing without belonging'. To describe our nation as unbelieving does not square with the evidence.

2. Psalm 73:1–5

3. Matthew 6:2, 5, 16; 15:7; 22:18; 23:13, 15, 23, 25, 27, 29

4. 1 Samuel 16:11

5. 1 Samuel 16:23

6. 1 Samuel 17:41–44

7. 1 Samuel 17:45–47

8. Mark 11:22–23

9. 1 Samuel 17:24

Chapter 5

1. Romans 8:28

2. Psalm 119:105

3. Colossians 3:15

4. Isaiah 30:15

5. Acts 4:13–31

6. 2 Chronicles 18:7

7. Acts 16:6

8. Acts 8:26–39

9. Acts 10:9–16; 11:4–18

10. Acts 18:9

11. Matthew 7:21

Chapter 6

1. 1 Samuel 17

2. 2 Samuel 11

3. Luke 4:4

4. Genesis 1:27

5. Philippians 4:11–13

Chapter 7

1. *Daily Telegraph*, 6 April 1996
2. C.S. Lewis, *A Grief Observed*, Faber & Faber Ltd, 1961, page 26
3. Romans 6:23

Chapter 8

1. René Descartes, *Le Discours de la Méthode*

Chapter 9

1. Karl Marx, *Kritik der Hegelschen Rechtsphilosophie*, Introduction
2. Psalm 23:4
3. 1 Peter 5:7

Chapter 10

1. Luke 19:5

Chapter 11

1. John 15:5
2. Galatians 5:22
3. Stephen R. Covey, *The Seven Habits of Highly Effective People*, Simon & Schuster, 1989

Chapter 12

1. Matthew 11:28
2. Psalm 139:14

Chapter 13

1. Galatians 6:7–8
2. Jonah 3:1

Chapter 14

1. Genesis 3:3
2. Ephesians 2:1
3. Genesis 3:8
4. Romans 6:23
5. 1 Corinthians 15:3
6. Justin 2, Apology 12, quoted in *Adam, Eve and the Serpent*, Elaine Pagell, Weidenfeld & Nicholson, 1988, page 36

Chapter 15

1. Acts 2:1–13

Chapter 16

1. Bruce Larsen, *Dare to Live Now*, Arthur James (Evesham), 1967, page 79
2. Mark 11:22
3. Psalm 119:89–90
4. *The Gospel, the Spirit and the Church*, Keswick Ministry, STL Books, 1976
5. James 1:22
6. Luke 17:5–6

Chapter 17

1. Job 3:11
2. Job 3:16
3. Job 3:20–21
4. Job 2:13
5. W.H. Auden, *Poems* (number 27), 1933
6. 1 Corinthians 13:11–12
7. Ken Blanchard, *The One Minute Manager builds High Performing Teams*, HarperCollins Business, 1994, page 27
8. Proverbs 19:21
9. Donald Sutherland, *Gertrude Stein: A Biography of her Works*, 1951, chapter 6
10. Psalm 13

Chapter 18

1. John Stott, *The Cross of Christ*, Inter-Varsity Press 1986, page 311
2. 2 Corinthians 11:23–25 (NIV)
3. 2 Corinthians 12:7–9
4. John Stott, *The Cross of Christ*, Inter-Varsity Press, 1986, pages 335–336

Chapter 19

1. Luke 11:11–13
2. Harry Blamires, *On Christian Truth*, SPCK, 1983, page 105
3. Psalm 121

Chapter 20

1. Genesis 2:15
2. Genesis 2:18
3. Genesis 3:17–19
4. Genesis 4:1–9
5. John 13:14
6. Matthew 20:16
7. Galatians 5:23
8. 1 Corinthians 12:27
9. 1 Corinthians 12:7
10. 1 Corinthians 12:12–13
11. Galatians 3:28
12. Stephen R. Covey, *The Seven Habits of Highly Effective People*, Simon & Schuster, 1989
13. Ken Blanchard, *The One Minute Manager builds High Performing Teams*, Harper Collins Business, 1994

Chapter 21

1. Bill Hybells, Stuart Briscoe and Haddon Robinson, *Mastering Contemporary Preaching*, Multnomah Press, 1989, page 23
2. Matthew 7:21
3. Stephen R. Covey, *The Seven Habits of Highly Effective People*, Simon & Schuster, 1989
4. See 1 Peter 1:7

Chapter 22

1. Psalm 119:105
2. 2 Timothy 3:16–17
3. Galatians 6:2
4. Hebrews 10:39
5. Hebrews 3:13 (NIV)
6. Hebrews 10:25 (NIV)
7. Robin Gamble, *The Irrelevant Church*, Monarch, 1991, page 11

Chapter 23

1. Genesis 1:26, 31
2. Romans 1:25

Chapter 24

1. Genesis 2:18
2. John 4:1–39
3. John 4:17–18
4. 1 John 4:10–11
5. The names have been changed to retain anonymity.
6. John 15:12
7. Ecclesiastes 4:12

Chapter 25

1. *Daily Mail*, 14 October 1996
2. Matthew 18:23–35
3. 1 Corinthians 15:3
4. Matthew 5:44
5. Colossians 3:13

Chapter 26

1. Psalm 51:1–2
2. *Daily Mail*, 14 October 1996
3. 1 Peter 2:24
4. Hebrews 9:14
5. Psalm 139:14

Chapter 27

1. John Stott, *The Cross of Christ*, IVP, 1986, page 334
2. Jonah 4:1
3. Jonah 4:2–4
4. Psalm 74:1; Psalm 10:1
5. William Temple, *Christus Veritas*, Macmillan, 1924, page 269
6. Job 9:23

Chapter 28

1. 1 Timothy 4:12
2. Matthew 7:24–27
3. T.S. Eliot, Choruses from 'The Rock', from *Collected Poems 1909–1962*, Faber and Faber Ltd
4. James 1:5–6

5. Proverbs 1:7

6. Reported in *The Times*, 17 December 1970

7. Richard Wightman, *Reinhold Niebuhr*, 1985, chapter 12

Chapter 29

1. 2 Corinthians 9:7

2. Acts 20:35

3. Philippians 2:6–8

4. Ephesians 1:13

5. Galatians 5:22

6. The name has been changed to retain anonymity.

Chapter 30

1. Michel Quoist, *The Christian Response*, Gill & McMillan, 1965

2. 1 Peter 5:7

3. Lee Strobel, *Inside the Mind of Unchurched Harry and Mary*, Zondervan, 1993

4. John 14:6

5. e.g. John 4

6. e.g. Mark 2:1–12